Horns and Hides

Horns and Hides

The Fascinating Anatomy of Rhinoceros Species

Solomon Raj

Spectra Enterprise

CONTENTS

INDEX

INTRODUCTION

In the tremendous and unpredictable woven artwork of the set of all animals, hardly any animals spellbind the creative mind very like the rhinoceros. Magnificent, strong, and covered in a demeanor of ancient persona, rhinos stand as notorious agents of Earth's biodiversity. Past their titanic height and tough qualities, it is the confounding designs on their heads - the horns - that have woven a story of interest, risk, and preservation.

The investigation of rhinoceros life systems divulges a story complicatedly connected to their developmental history, geographic circulation, and social importance. From the savannas of Africa to the thick wildernesses of Asia, rhinos explore a reality where endurance is a sensitive dance among transformation and the constant tensions of human effect. As we dig into the profundities of their life systems, we disentangle the actual wonders that characterize rhinos as well as the complicated difficulties they face in a quickly impacting world.

Disclosing the Rhinoceros Genealogy

The excursion into the life structures of rhinoceros species starts with an investigation of their transformative history. Rhinos, having a place with the Perissodactyla request, share a different genealogical record that stretches across landmasses and ages. From the wooly rhinoceros of the Pleistocene to the surviving white and dark rhinos of Africa and the one-horned and two-horned rhinos of Asia, the rhinoceros family brags a rich embroidery animal groups with extraordinary transformations sharpened by a long period of time of development.

This part digs into the fossil records and hereditary investigations that have uncovered the unpredictable parts of the rhinoceros genealogy. It investigates the versatile methodologies that permitted rhinos to flourish in different conditions and the particular tensions that molded their unmistakable morphological elements. From perusing progenitors to the specific nibblers of today, understanding the transformative excursion of rhinoceros species establishes the groundwork for fathoming the subtleties of their life structures.

Planning the Regions - Geographic Dispersion of Rhinoceros Species

The immense scenes of Africa and Asia act as the stage for the following part in our investigation - the geographic conveyance of rhinoceros species. Every species has cut a specialty inside its particular territory, adjusting to the extraordinary difficulties and valuable open doors introduced by the differed biological systems they call home.

This part leaves on an excursion across the savannas, prairies, and backwoods that structure the background of rhinoceros regions. It disentangles the elements impacting their conveyance, from biological inclinations and dietary variations to the vital job they play as cornerstone species in molding their surroundings.

As we navigate the geological embroidery of rhinos, we experience the sensitive harmony between human networks and these wonderful animals, an equilibrium that, when upset, presents huge dangers to their endurance.

Past Shallow - Morphology and Actual Qualities

The life structures of rhinoceros species stretches out a long ways past what meets the eye. In this part, we strip back the layers, investigating the unpredictable subtleties of their morphology and actual attributes. From the interesting construction of their appendages to the unmistakable shapes and sizes of their horns, rhinos have developed to epitomize an amicable mix of structure and capability.

The assessment of rhino morphology divulges the variations that prepare them for endurance in their particular natural surroundings. Tough qualities, described by a shield like quality, give assurance against ecological components and expected hunters. Appendages intended for quick development and strong charges exhibit the transformative arrangements that have permitted rhinos to explore different scenes. This section offers a complete picture of the actual qualities that characterize rhinoceros life structures, displaying the resourcefulness of nature's plan.

The General Body Design - An Ensemble of Variations

Expanding upon the investigation of morphology, this section digs into the general body construction of rhinoceros species. It disentangles the complexities of their skeletal and strong frameworks, every component finely tuned to satisfy the needs of their special ways of life. From the vigorous casing of the white rhinoceros, worked for brushing on the African fields, to the deft height of the Sumatran rhinoceros, adjusted for life in thick timberlands, the variety of their body structures mirrors the versatile splendor of advancement.

Understanding the general body structure goes past the shallow assessment of life systems; it opens a window into the social environment of rhinos. From social designs and correspondence to taking care of propensities and conceptive systems, the body structure fills in as a material whereupon the narrative of rhinoceros life is painted. This part unfurls the orchestra of transformations that permit rhinos to flourish in their separate living spaces, displaying the finely tuned agreement between their structure and capability.

Appendage Life systems and Transformations - The Craft of Movement

The capacity to move nimbly and quickly is a characterizing component of rhinoceros life systems. Appendage life systems and variations assume a vital part in their versatility, impacting their scrounging techniques, regional developments, and reactions to possible dangers.

From the strong steps of the white rhinoceros to the deft route of thick vegetation by the Javan rhinoceros, appendage life systems is a demonstration of the variety of methodologies utilized by rhinos to explore their surroundings.

This section takes apart the complexities of appendage life systems, investigating variations, for example, foot structure, joint adaptability, and solid strength. It analyzes the job of appendages in ways of behaving going from regional stamping to romance ceremonies, revealing insight into the multi-layered meaning of appendage life systems in the existences of rhinoceros species.

A More critical Glance at Skin - Qualities and Tinge

Underneath the rough outside of rhinoceros conceals lies a universe of captivating qualities and hues. This section dives into the complexities of rhino skin, from its piece and surface to the job it plays in thermoregulation, correspondence, and cover. The apparently impervious reinforcement of rhino stows away disguises a dynamic and flexible organ that serves a large number of capabilities.

Investigating the tinge of rhino skin uncovers tasteful varieties as well as useful transformations. From the dark protective layer of the white rhinoceros, mixing consistently with the dusty savannas, to the finished and overlap rich skin of the Indian rhinoceros, disguise and thermoregulation are woven into the actual texture of their stows away. This part welcomes perusers to peer underneath the surface and value the multifaceted universe of rhino skin, a central member in their step by step processes for surviving.

Horns and Their Importance - Nature's Ivory

Horns, the famous enhancements that crown the heads of rhinoceroses, stand as the two images of nature's greatness and harbingers of danger. This part leaves on a top to bottom investigation of rhino horns - their organization, development, and the complex jobs they play in the existences of these heavenly animals. From the singular, prolonged horn of the Indian rhinoceros to the matched, powerful horns of the African white rhinoceros, every variety recounts a one of a kind story of transformation and natural reason.

The meaning of rhino horns reaches out past their actual presence; they are vital to rhino conduct, correspondence, and even mate choice. This part discloses the intricacies of horn elements, from the development designs impacted by age and species to the strange appeal that has energized request in unlawful natural life exchange. As we disentangle the layers of importance, we go up against the protection challenges attached to the poaching emergency that undermines rhino populaces.

Past the Savannahs - Stows away and Cover

The stows away of rhinoceroses, however frequently eclipsed by the unmistakable quality of their horns, hold insider facts vital for their endurance. In this section, we adventure past the savannahs and investigate the complicated universe of rhino stows away and their part in cover. From the rough protection of the white rhinoceros, flawlessly mixing with the dry scenes, to the thick and collapsed stows away of the Javan rhinoceros, disguise is a crucial part of their biological techniques.

This investigation reaches out to the interaction among stows away and ecological elements, for example, vegetation and lighting conditions, that shape the adequacy of rhino disguise. The stows away, decorated with one of a kind examples and surfaces, go about as both defensive safeguards and vital devices for staying away from hunters and expected dangers. As we dig into the lesser-investigated domain of rhino stows away, we unwind the nuanced variations that add to their endurance in different environments.

1. **Overview of rhinoceros species**

The rhinoceros, an animal of both earthly may and ancient charm, remains as a demonstration of the rich biodiversity of our planet. This outline takes us on an excursion through the different embroidery of rhinoceros species, investigating their extraordinary qualities, living spaces, and the squeezing protection challenges that undermine their reality.

1. **The African Monsters: White Rhinoceros (Ceratotherium simum) and Dark Rhinoceros (Diceros bicornis)**

   The African landmass is home to two magnificent rhinoceros species - the White Rhinoceros (Ceratotherium simum) and the Dark Rhinoceros (Diceros bicornis). In spite of their names, the qualification between these species did not depend on variety yet rather on the state of their mouths. The white rhino, with its expansive, square-molded mouth, is very much adjusted for nibbling on grasses. Interestingly, the dark rhino, including a snared upper lip, is prepared for perusing on bushes and trees.

   The White Rhinoceros, the bigger of the two, is partitioned into two subspecies - the Southern White Rhinoceros and the fundamentally imperiled Northern White Rhinoceros. By and large, the Southern White Rhino has been a protection example of overcoming adversity, with purposeful endeavors prompting populace recuperations in nations like South Africa. The Northern White Rhino, be that as it may, wavers near the very edge of elimination, with a couple of people staying in bondage.

   The Dark Rhinoceros, once far reaching across Africa, has confronted a serious downfall essentially because of poaching for its sought after horn. While preservation drives have gained ground in settling a few populaces, challenges endure, and the dark rhino stays delegated basically imperiled.

2. **The Indian Rhinoceros (Rhinoceros unicornis): A Gem of the Subcontinent**
In the rich scenes of the Indian subcontinent, the Indian Rhinoceros (Rhinoceros unicornis) orders consideration with its single horn and powerful form. Found in the prairies and marshes of India and Nepal, this species has become inseparable from the biodiversity of the area. The Indian rhino is recognized by its protective layer like skin folds, which make a particular example across its body.

Preservation endeavors, especially in India's Kaziranga Public Park, have been instrumental in the recuperation of Indian rhinoceros populaces. Nonetheless, dangers, for example, territory misfortune and human-natural life struggle persevere, stressing the continuous requirement for cautious protection measures.

3. **The Sumatran Rhinoceros (Dicerorhinus sumatrensis): An Evaporating Symbol of Southeast Asia**
In the thick rainforests of Southeast Asia, the tricky Sumatran Rhinoceros (Dicerorhinus sumatrensis) explores a scene laden with difficulties. As the littlest and hairiest of all rhino species, the Sumatran rhino is furnished with interesting variations, including a rosy earthy colored layer of hair and two little horns.

This species faces a basic status near the precarious edge of termination, fundamentally because of environment misfortune and discontinuity. With little and divided populaces in Indonesia and Malaysia, the Sumatran rhinoceros is quite possibly of the most extraordinary enormous vertebrate on The planet. Preservation endeavors center around safeguarding and interfacing their excess natural surroundings, as well as hostage rearing drives pointed toward supporting their numbers.

4. **The Javan Rhinoceros (Rhinoceros sondaicus): A Problematic Presence in Java**
Endemic to the island of Java in Indonesia, the Javan Rhinoceros (Rhinoceros sondaicus) possesses a one of a kind natural specialty. Unmistakable by its single horn and moderately little size, the Javan rhino is one of the most imperiled huge vertebrates internationally, with a populace bound to Ujung Kulon Public Park. Territory misfortune and authentic hunting have radically diminished the Javan rhinoceros populace. Preservation endeavors focus on living space assurance, against poaching measures, and local area commitment to get the fate of this basically imperiled species.

5. **The White Rhinoceros: A Preservation Achievement and Progressing Difficulties**
The Southern White Rhinoceros (Ceratotherium simum), a sub-types of the White Rhinoceros, has arisen as an encouraging sign in the domain of rhinoceros protection. When near the precarious edge of termination, especially

in South Africa, purposeful endeavors have prompted populace recuperations, making the Southern White Rhino the most various rhino species.

Assurance in devoted stores and hostile to poaching measures play played vital parts in the protection outcome of the Southern White Rhino. Be that as it may, the shadow of poaching actually poses a potential threat, filled by the interest for rhino horn in unlawful business sectors. Progressing carefulness and inventive protection methodologies are fundamental for secure the additions made and guarantee the proceeded with endurance of this tough species.

6. **The Basic Intersection: Preservation Difficulties and Dangers**

Regardless of the flexibility of specific rhinoceros populaces, all species face an unfavorable apparition - the raising danger of poaching. The interest for rhino horns, driven by customary convictions and a flourishing underground market, represents a grave risk to these notable animals. Poaching imperils individual rhinos as well as sabotages the fragile equilibrium of environments and disturbs the interconnected trap of biodiversity.

Environment misfortune and discontinuity arise as extra difficulties, especially for species like the Sumatran and Javan rhinoceroses. Quick urbanization, horticultural extension, and infrastructural advancement infringe upon their normal territories, leaving rhinos disengaged and powerless.

Human-untamed life struggle further confounds preservation endeavors. As human populaces grow and encroach upon rhino domains, conflicts emerge, frequently bringing about damage to the two people and rhinos. Maintainable arrangements that orchestrate the conjunction of networks and rhinoceros populaces are basic for long haul achievement.

7. **Preservation Drives: Defending What's in store**

Even with overwhelming difficulties, an orchestra of protection drives resonates across the globe. Against poaching measures, including the organization of talented officers, mechanical advancements, and global cooperation, structure the vanguard of endeavors to safeguard rhinoceros populaces.

Local area based protection programs connect with neighborhood inhabitants as stewards of rhino natural surroundings, cultivating a feeling of shared liability. Economical occupation open doors and instructive drives make a harmonious connection between human prosperity and rhino preservation.

Environment reclamation projects expect to recover corrupted scenes, making passages to reconnect divided regions. Movement and renewed introduction programs offer expect modifying populaces in regions where rhinos have been extirpated.

Examination and checking drives, utilizing mechanical progressions, give basic experiences into rhino conduct, hereditary qualities, and wellbeing. This information illuminates proof based protection techniques, guaranteeing versatile administration and the improvement of assets.

8. The Street Ahead: An Aggregate Source of inspiration

As we study the different scene of rhinoceros species, it becomes obvious that their endurance is a common obligation that rises above lines and limits. The protection venture requires an aggregate responsibility from states, networks, non-legislative associations, specialists, and worldwide residents.

The street ahead requests creative arrangements, constant watchfulness, and a change in outlook in perspectives toward natural life and protection. Training and mindfulness drives, dispersing fantasies encompassing rhino items and encouraging compassion, assume a critical part in forming values and ways of behaving.

Global coordinated effort remains as a key part in the battle against unlawful natural life exchange. Fortifying lawful structures, upgrading implementation measures, and strategic endeavors are necessary parts of a worldwide reaction to a worldwide test.

B. Importance of understanding rhinoceros anatomy

In the multifaceted trap of Earth's biodiversity, the rhinoceros remains as an image of solidarity, versatility, and transformative splendor. Past its spectacular actual presence, diving into the profundities of rhinoceros life systems isn't only a practice in stylish interest; it is a pivotal undertaking with broad ramifications for preservation, environmental equilibrium, and our aggregate liability as stewards of the regular world.

1. Preservation Basic: A Profound Plunge into Rhino Science

Understanding rhinoceros life systems is major to the protection basic that highlights the endurance of these notorious species. The life structures of rhinos is unpredictably connected to their ways of behaving, conceptive methodologies, and biological jobs. By disentangling the subtleties of their life structures, traditionalists gain experiences into the variables impacting populace elements and the particular requirements fundamental for their prosperity.

A far reaching handle of rhinoceros life structures helps with the improvement of designated preservation procedures. From hostile to poaching measures custom fitted to safeguard indispensable physical elements like horns to natural surroundings reclamation drives that think about the particular biological necessities of various rhino species, a nuanced comprehension of their life systems illuminates choices that can have the effect between populace decline and recuperation.

Besides, even with arising dangers, for example, environmental change and territory fracture, understanding rhinoceros life systems turns into a compass for versatile preservation. The versatility of rhino populaces notwithstanding ecological difficulties is unpredictably attached to their physiological transformations. By understanding these variations, progressives can foresee and moderate the effects of a changing environment on rhino living spaces, guaranteeing the proceeded with endurance of these sublime animals.

2. **Unwinding the Secrets of Development: Rhinoceros Genealogical record**

   The investigation of rhinoceros life systems fills in as a key to open the secrets of their transformative excursion. Rhinos, having a place with the request Perissodactyla, share a different genealogy that stretches across landmasses and ages. Investigating the morphological transformations carved in their life systems gives hints to the specific tensions that formed their developmental direction.

   From the genealogical wooly rhinoceros that meandered the Pleistocene scenes to the surviving white and dark rhinos of Africa and the one-horned and two-horned rhinos of Asia, each part of the rhinoceros genealogy recounts an account of transformation to different conditions. Understanding the transformative history encoded in their life systems improves our insight into Earth's biodiversity as well as establishes the groundwork for viable protection by perceiving the one of a kind variations that empower rhinos to flourish in unambiguous environments.

3. **Geographic Conveyance: Life structures With regards to Environments**

   The geographic conveyance of rhinoceros species is personally associated with their life structures, as various species have advanced explicit transformations to flourish in particular living spaces. Investigating the life systems of rhinos with regards to their territories offers important experiences into the environmental specialties they possess and the exceptional difficulties they face in assorted scenes.

   For instance, the white rhinoceros, adjusted for nibbling with its wide, square-molded mouth, rules the green savannas of Africa. Conversely, the dark rhinoceros, furnished with a snared upper lip for perusing, explores the difficulties of bush rich scenes. Understanding these physical variations gives a focal point through which traditionalists can tailor methodologies to safeguard and save the environments fundamental for every rhinoceros species.

   The geographic dispersion of rhinos isn't static; it is a powerful exchange impacted by variables, for example, environmental change, human exercises, and natural movements. By grasping the life systems of rhinos with regards to their evolving natural surroundings, protection endeavors can proactively address the difficulties presented by moving scenes, guaranteeing the strength of rhino populaces despite ecological motion.

4. **Morphology and Actual Attributes: Bits of knowledge into Conduct and Biology**

   The investigation of rhinoceros life structures reaches out past the shallow to divulge the complexities of their morphology and actual qualities. From the hearty casing of the white rhinoceros worked for brushing on the African fields to the dexterous height of the Sumatran rhinoceros adjusted for life in thick woods, every species conveys a one of a kind arrangement of morphological elements that shape its way of behaving and nature.

The tough qualities, described by a defensive layer like quality, give security against ecological components and possible hunters. Appendages intended for quick development and strong charges feature the transformative arrangements that have permitted rhinos to explore different scenes. Understanding the morphology and actual qualities of rhinos offers an all encompassing perspective on their transformations, revealing insight into their taking care of propensities, social designs, and regenerative methodologies.

For example, the particular overlays and examples on rhino stows away are not just stylish; they fill utilitarian needs like thermoregulation and cover. Appendage structure impacts portability, regional developments, and collaborations inside rhino populaces. A profound plunge into these parts of rhinoceros life structures gives a nuanced comprehension of their ways of behaving, empowering moderates to plan mediations that regard the regular senses and natural jobs of these superb animals.

5. **Appendage Life structures and Variations: The Specialty of Movement**

   Appendage life structures is a basic part of rhinoceros science, impacting their portability, rummaging systems, and reactions to likely dangers. The capacity to move nimbly and quickly is a characterizing element of rhinoceros life structures, forming their collaborations with the climate and different individuals from their species.

   The strong steps of the white rhinoceros, adjusted for covering immense distances in open savannas, mirror an appendage structure streamlined for productive movement. Conversely, the deft route of thick vegetation by the Javan rhinoceros features variations that consider spryness in additional bound spaces. Appendage life structures likewise assumes an essential part in rhino ways of behaving like regional stamping, romance ceremonies, and reactions to saw dangers. Understanding these variations gives critical experiences into the natural jobs of rhinos inside their environments and helps in the detailing of preservation systems that think about the unique exchange between appendage life structures and conduct.

6. **A More critical Glance at Skin: Qualities and Tinge**

   Underneath the rough outside of rhinoceros conceals lies a universe of captivating qualities and hues. The apparently invulnerable defensive layer of rhino stows away hides a dynamic and flexible organ that serves a large number of capabilities. Understanding the qualities and hues of rhino skin goes past tasteful appreciation; it digs into the practical variations that add to their step by step processes for surviving.

   The structure and surface of rhino skin assume a part in thermoregulation, with folds and wrinkles supporting intensity dissemination in hotter environments. The hue of rhino skin, frequently fluctuating from species to species, fills both stylish and biological needs. The dim protection of the white rhinoceros, mixing consistently with the dusty savannas, gives powerful disguise, while the finished and crease rich skin of the Indian rhinoceros fills in as a particular element.

The interchange between skin attributes and shading stretches out to the domain of correspondence. Fragrance checking ways of behaving, worked with by particular organs in the skin, pass on data about regions, conceptive status, and individual personality. Understanding these complex parts of rhino skin adds to an all encompassing cognizance of their science and conduct, directing protection endeavors that recognize the significance of this diverse organ.

7. **Horns and Their Importance: Nature's Ivory**

The notorious decorations that crown the heads of rhinoceroses - their horns - stand as the two images of nature's loftiness and harbingers of danger. An intensive comprehension of the life structures and meaning of rhino horns is fundamental for tending to the mind boggling difficulties presented by unlawful natural life exchange, living space protection, and the multifaceted elements of rhino populaces.

Rhino horns are not simple tasteful limbs; they assume crucial parts in rhino conduct, correspondence, and mate choice. The development examples of horns, impacted by elements like age and species, add to the singular personality of rhinos. Horns are likewise instrumental in regional denoting, a way of behaving that lays out and builds up limits inside rhino populaces.

Past their environmental capabilities, rhino horns have been pushed into the spotlight because of the raising interest driven by customary convictions and the illegal market for their implied restorative properties. The unlawful exchange rhino horns represents a serious danger to rhino populaces, prompting boundless poaching and populace declines. A top to bottom comprehension of horn life structures and importance is urgent for creating viable protection procedures that address the underlying drivers of poaching and defend the fate of rhinoceros species.

8. **Past the Savannahs: Stows away and Cover**

While horns frequently become the overwhelming focus, the stows away of rhinoceroses harbor privileged insights vital for their endurance. Past the savannas, where the rough protective layer of the white rhinoceros mixes consistently with dry scenes, conceals assume a urgent part in the cover and biological procedures of rhino species.

The complicated universe of rhino stows away, portrayed by remarkable examples and surfaces, goes about as both a defensive safeguard and an essential instrument for staying away from hunters and expected dangers. The stows away of rhinos, embellished with varieties in variety and surface, are tasteful wonders as well as versatile highlights sharpened by advancement. Grasping the exchange among stows away and ecological variables, like vegetation and lighting conditions, gives bits of knowledge into the adequacy of rhino disguise in various scenes.

The meaning of stows away stretches out past visual disguise. The finished surfaces of rhino stows away add to thermoregulation, supporting intensity dissemination in hotter environments. The folds and wrinkles of their stows away likewise assume a part in correspondence, with fragrance checking ways of behaving passing on critical data about domains and conceptive status.

As preservation endeavors endeavor to get the living spaces of rhino populaces, understanding the mind boggling connection among stows away and disguise becomes instrumental. Safeguarding scenes that offer normal cover and mixing open doors is essential for the proceeded with progress of rhinoceros species in nature.

C. Purpose of the book: Explore the intricacies of horns and hides in rhinoceroses

The motivation behind "Horns and Stows away: The Entrancing Life systems of Rhinoceros Species" stretches out a long ways past the domain of a simple investigation. It is an excursion into the core of the regular world, a careful unwinding of the complexities that characterize the famous rhinoceros - an animal that stands at the junction of dazzling brilliance and critical preservation concern. This book tries to dive profound into the double ponders of horns and stows away, enlightening the subtleties of their life systems, importance, and the convincing accounts they wind in the more extensive embroidered artwork of Earth's biodiversity.

1. **Crossing over Science and Marvel: An All encompassing Investigation**

   At its center, the book looks to connect the domains of logical request and marvel, welcoming perusers into the entrancing universe of rhinoceros life systems. The investigation of horns and conceals fills in as an entryway to understanding the unpredictable plan rules that have molded these glorious animals north of millions of years. By wedding logical meticulousness with open language, the book expects to demystify complex physical ideas, offering a story that both draws in and teaches.

   The complexities of rhinoceros life structures are not restricted to reading material and examination papers; they are dynamic stories ready to be told. Through this book, perusers are welcome to set out on an excursion that reveals the developmental history scratched in rhino qualities, the variations finely tuned to different conditions, and the enrapturing stories murmured by horns and stows away. An investigation tries to light interest, invigorate wonder, and encourage a more profound appreciation for the wonders of the regular world.

2. **Preservation Cognizance: A Call to Safeguard Symbols of Versatility**

   Implanted inside the pages of the book is a resonating call for preservation cognizance. Rhinoceroses, with their radiant horns and stows away, have become representative figures of regular magnificence as well as of the dire requirement for protection. The book tries to reveal insight into the basic preservation challenges looked by rhino populaces internationally, especially the unavoidable danger of poaching driven by the interest for rhino horns.

By disentangling the meaning of rhino horns - from their parts in correspondence to the social and emblematic aspects - the book plans to cultivate a sympathetic comprehension of these animals' situation. It fills in as a clarion call to perusers, encouraging them to perceive the interconnectedness of human activities with the destiny of rhinoceroses. The object isn't simply to illuminate yet to electrify people, networks, and worldwide residents into aggregate activity to safeguard these symbols of flexibility.

3. **A Thorough Reference: Exploring the Embroidery of Rhinoceros Variety**
"Horns and Stows away" tries to be in excess of a dazzling read; it plans to act as an exhaustive reference on the variety of rhinoceros species. The book explores the peruser through the rich embroidered artwork of rhino science, presenting the unmistakable qualities of African goliaths like the white and dark rhinoceroses, the Asian diamonds like the Indian and Sumatran rhinoceroses, and the fundamentally imperiled Javan rhinoceros.

Through definite investigations of their morphological highlights, geographic disseminations, and natural jobs, the book builds a comprehensive representation of every rhino species.

It turns into an aide for devotees, understudies, and scientists looking for a more profound comprehension of the subtleties that separate one animal types from another. This thorough methodology enables perusers with information, encouraging a feeling of association with these noteworthy creatures and a pledge to their conservation.

4. **Logical Request: Opening Developmental Accounts**
Logical interest is the motor that impels the account of "Horns and Stows away." The book is created as an instrument for opening the developmental stories engraved in rhinoceros qualities. Perusers are directed through the passageways of time, following the rhino genealogical record from the wooly rhinoceros of the Pleistocene to the surviving white, dark, Indian, Sumatran, and Javan rhinoceroses.

This logical request stretches out to the morphology, actual qualities, and transformations that have permitted rhinoceroses to overcome different living spaces. The object is to offer perusers a brief look into the mind boggling dance among hereditary qualities and climate, displaying how rhinos have shaped their life systems to become wonderful survivors across mainlands and environments. The book tries to light the flash of logical interest, welcoming perusers to become stewards of information and heroes of protection.

5. **Horns Revealed: Development, Reason, and Human Association**
Horns, the delegated greatness of rhinoceroses, become the overwhelming focus in this investigation. The book strips back the layers of secret encompassing rhino horns, uncovering the development designs affected by age and species.

It dives into the natural elements of horns, like correspondence and regional stamping, displaying them as elaborate highlights as well as necessary parts of rhino conduct and step by step processes for surviving.

A critical part of the book's motivation is to explain the mind boggling connection between rhino horns and human association. The interest for rhino horns, driven by conventional convictions and the unlawful natural life exchange, represents a grave danger to rhino populaces. By looking at the authentic importance, social aspects, and the protection challenges attached to rhino horns, the book prompts perusers to think about the job of humankind in both the hazard and safeguarding of these grand animals.

6. **Stows away Exposed: Cover, Correspondence, and Preservation Difficulties**
The stows away of rhinoceroses, frequently eclipsed by the conspicuousness of their horns, get a spotlight in this investigation. The book disentangles the mysteries concealed inside rhino stows away, investigating their part in cover, thermoregulation, and correspondence.

By analyzing the multifaceted connection among stows away and ecological elements, the book reveals insight into the versatile systems that add to the endurance of rhinoceros species in assorted environments.

In addition, the investigation of stows away uncovers the protection challenges weaved with their conservation. As scenes change because of human exercises, understanding the job of conceals in the environmental systems of rhinos becomes pivotal for making protection drives that shield their natural surroundings. The design isn't just to commend the tasteful variety of rhino stows away however to highlight their useful importance notwithstanding contemporary preservation challenges.

7. **Preservation Accounts: From Difficulties to Arrangements**
At its center, "Horns and Stows away" is a protection story that faces the moves undermining rhinoceros populaces and looks to diagram a course toward arrangements. The book fills in as a stage for examining the diverse issues of poaching, natural surroundings misfortune, environmental change, and human-untamed life struggle. It doesn't avoid the unmistakable real factors yet defies them with an immovable obligation to promotion and mindfulness.

Every part unfurls as a source of inspiration, welcoming perusers to draw in with the protection story, add to hostile to poaching endeavors, support territory reclamation undertakings, and champion reasonable concurrence among people and rhinos. By introducing the difficulties close by examples of overcoming adversity, the book means to rouse a feeling of organization and strengthening among its perusers, encouraging an aggregate ethos of obligation toward the conservation of rhinoceros species.

8. **Instructive Asset: Supporting an Age of Protectionists**

Past its job as an enamoring story, "Horns and Stows away" tries to be an instructive asset that sustains an age of preservationists. The book is intended to be open to a different crowd, from understudies and teachers to natural life fans and policymakers. It tries to ingrain an energy for natural life preservation, offering a window into the unpredictable universe of rhinoceros life structures that fills in as a door to more extensive biological comprehension.

In study halls, the book can be a device for encouraging interest, decisive reasoning, and a feeling of natural stewardship. Its motivation isn't just to spread data yet to encourage the fire of promotion inside the personalities of future protection pioneers. By giving a far reaching asset on rhinoceros life systems, "Horns and Stows away" expects to add to a more educated and connected with worldwide local area effectively put resources into the insurance of our planet's biodiversity.

Chapter 1

The Rhinoceros Family

The rhinoceros family, deductively known as Rhinocerotidae, addresses a remarkable and sensational genealogy of animals that have caught the interest of the two researchers and nature devotees the same. In this exhaustive investigation, we leave on an excursion to figure out the developmental history, ordered grouping, and geographic dispersion of these grand creatures.

Developmental History of Rhinoceroses

To appreciate the intricacies of the rhinoceros family, one must initially dig into their transformative history. Rhinoceroses have a place with the request Perissodactyla, which likewise incorporates ponies and ungulates. Fossil proof follows the starting points of the rhinoceros family back to the Eocene age, roughly a long time back. The developmental way of rhinoceroses has been set apart by transformations to evolving conditions, bringing about the assorted species we notice today.

Scientific categorization and Grouping

The scientific classification of the rhinoceros family is a significant part of grasping their spot in the set of all animals. At present, there are five surviving species inside the family Rhinocerotidae: the White Rhinoceros (Ceratotherium simum), the Dark Rhinoceros (Diceros bicornis), the Indian Rhinoceros (Rhinoceros unicornis), the Javan Rhinoceros (Rhinoceros sondaicus), and the Sumatran Rhinoceros (Dicerorhinus sumatrensis).

These species are additionally sorted into three genera: Ceratotherium, Diceros, and Rhinoceros. Every sort incorporates particular qualities that add to the general variety inside the rhinoceros family.

Geographic Conveyance of Rhinoceros Species

Rhinoceroses display a boundless geographic dispersion, adjusting to different biological systems across Africa and Asia. The White Rhinoceros, for example, is basically tracked down in savannas and meadows of southern Africa, while the Dark

Rhinoceros possesses a more different scope of conditions, including fields, savannas, and woodlands.

In Asia, the Indian Rhinoceros flourishes in the prairies and marshes of the Indian subcontinent, while the Javan Rhinoceros is basically jeopardized and restricted to explicit areas in Java. The Sumatran Rhinoceros, confronting what is going on, is tracked down in disconnected pockets of Southeast Asia.

Significance of Morphology and Actual Attributes

The morphology and actual qualities of rhinoceroses assume a vital part in their transformation to different conditions. Understanding the general body structure, appendage life systems, and skin qualities gives bits of knowledge into their transformative excursion and step by step processes for surviving.

General Body Design

Rhinoceroses are portrayed by their vigorous form and thick, defensive skin. They have an unmistakable appearance with a couple of conspicuous horns on their noses, which are made out of keratin — a similar protein tracked down in human hair and nails. The size and state of these horns fluctuate among species, adding to their novel tasteful allure.

Appendage Life systems and Transformations

The appendages of rhinoceroses are very much adjusted to their particular territories. Whether exploring the open prairies or crossing thick woods, their appendages give security and strength. The rhinoceros' three-toed feet are outfitted with hooves that guide in crossing different landscapes, displaying their transformative variations for endurance.

Skin Attributes and Hue

The skin of rhinoceroses fills numerous needs, going about as a defensive obstruction against outer components and expected hunters. The skin is much of the time thick and folds into unmistakable examples, giving an extra layer of guard. The shading of the skin fluctuates among species, going from the grayish tints of the White Rhinoceros to the hazier tones of the Dark Rhinoceros, considering successful cover in their particular surroundings.

Horns and Their Importance

One of the most notorious elements of rhinoceroses is their horns, which have accumulated both interest and dangerous consideration. Understanding the various sorts of rhinoceros horns, their development designs, and their capabilities is fundamental to valuing their importance in the more extensive setting of rhinoceros science.

Various Kinds of Rhinoceros Horns

Rhinoceros species display varieties in the number and state of their horns. The White Rhinoceros, for example, normally has two square-molded horns, while the Dark Rhinoceros might have a couple, with a more snared appearance. The Javan Rhinoceros, then again, commonly has a solitary horn.

Development and Advancement of Horns

The development and advancement of rhinoceros horns are interesting cycles impacted by elements like age, hereditary qualities, and natural circumstances. Horns are absent upon entering the world but rather start to arise without further ado subsequently. As the rhinoceros develops, so does the size and state of its horns, with consistent development all through its life.

Usefulness and Reason for Horns

Rhinoceros horns serve different capabilities, both in the wild and, sadly, as objects of want in unlawful exchanges. The main role of these horns is frequently connected with safeguard, as rhinoceroses use them to avoid possible dangers. Moreover, during social collaborations, horns assume a part in laying out predominance inside the populace.

Horns and Human Connection

The verifiable meaning of rhinoceros horns has profound roots in human culture and custom. Over the entire course of time, these horns have been loved for their apparent restorative properties, prompting a sad interest that energizes the unlawful exchange and poaching of rhinoceroses.

Verifiable Meaning of Rhinoceros Horns

Rhinoceros horns have been pursued for a really long time, esteemed for their alleged restorative properties and as superficial points of interest. In certain societies, these horns are ground into powder and utilized in conventional medication, in spite of the absence of logical proof supporting their viability. The authentic utilization of rhinoceros horns has added to the hazardous circumstance numerous rhinoceros species face today.

Social and Emblematic Significance

Past their therapeutic worth, rhinoceros horns hold social and representative importance in different social orders. They are much of the time used to make mind boggling ancient rarities and images of force or security. Investigating the social discernments and customs encompassing rhinoceros horns gives significant bits of knowledge into the mind boggling connection among people and these eminent animals.

Preservation Difficulties Connected with Horn Exchange

The unlawful exchange of rhinoceros horns stays a huge danger to their endurance. Poaching for the unlawful natural life exchange, driven by the interest for horns, has prompted an extraordinary decrease in rhinoceros populaces around the world. Protection endeavors face the test of controling this unlawful exchange while at the same time tending to the financial elements that drive poaching.

Stows away and Disguise

While horns characterize the appealling appearance of rhinoceroses, their conceals assume a similarly essential part in their endurance. The construction and hue of rhinoceros stows away are unpredictably connected to their capacity to flourish in different conditions through compelling disguise and assurance.

Skin Design and Structure

Rhinoceros conceals brag a one of a kind construction and piece that adds to their versatility. The thick and collapsed skin gives a characteristic safeguard against outside dangers, including the chomps of bugs and the unforgiving beams of the sun. Understanding the minuscule complexities of rhinoceros skin reveals insight into its defensive abilities.

Versatile Hue for Various Conditions

The hue of rhinoceros stows away isn't just an issue of style; it serves a vital job in their endurance. Various species show varieties in variety, permitting them to mix consistently into their separate natural surroundings. From the grayish-white tint of the White Rhinoceros, fit to open meadows, to the hazier shades of the Dark Rhinoceros, adjusted for changed scenes, these transformations feature the developmental brightness of rhinoceros cover.

Job of Conceals in Rhinoceros Endurance

Past disguise, rhinoceros conceals assume a vital part in their general endurance. The skin gives protection against temperature limits, supports controlling internal heat level, and goes about as a tangible organ. Understanding the complex elements of rhinoceros stows away divulges the complexities of their transformation to assorted environments.

Correspondence Through Non-verbal communication

Rhinoceroses are not singular animals; they participate in complex social designs that depend vigorously on correspondence through non-verbal communication. Noticing their ways of behaving and associations gives significant experiences into their social elements and supports the significance of preservation endeavors that save these complex connections.

Figuring out Rhinoceros Conduct

Rhinoceros conduct is set apart by a scope of communications, from lone scrounging to collective vibes inside a populace. Figuring out their ways of behaving, like brushing designs, mating ceremonies, and regional presentations, is fundamental for progressives trying to safeguard these creatures and their territories.

Meaning of Non-verbal communication in Correspondence

Correspondence among rhinoceroses is dominatingly non-verbal, depending on non-verbal communication to pass on messages. Stances, signals, and vocalizations assume key parts in communicating predominance, accommodation, or alerts inside the gathering. Unraveling the nuances of rhinoceros non-verbal communication improves how we might interpret their mind boggling social designs.

Associations Inside Rhinoceros Social Designs

Rhinoceros populaces display assorted social designs, fluctuating among species. While certain species, similar to the White Rhinoceros, may frame free gatherings, others, similar to the Dark Rhinoceros, are more lone in nature. Investigating these social elements offers a brief look into the complex connections that add to the general prosperity of rhinoceros populaces.

Conceptive Life structures

The continuation of the rhinoceros family depends on the complexities of their conceptive life structures. Looking at the conceptive organs, mating ways of behaving, and parental consideration gives an all encompassing comprehension of their life cycles and the difficulties they face in supporting solid populaces.

Regenerative Organs and Cycles

Rhinoceroses, in the same way as other well evolved creatures, have particular conceptive organs and cycles. Female rhinoceroses experience estrous cycles, during which they are open to mating. Understanding the regenerative life systems and cycles is fundamental for traditionalists looking to help regular reproducing ways of behaving in safeguarded conditions.

Romance and Mating Ways of behaving

The romance and mating ways of behaving of rhinoceroses include perplexing customs and presentations. From vocalizations to actual connections, these ways of behaving are fundamental for effective proliferation. Investigating the subtleties of romance reveals insight into the intricacy of rhinoceros connections.

Parental Consideration and Raising Posterity

Raising posterity is a cooperative exertion inside rhinoceros populaces. Inspecting parental consideration ways of behaving, for example, assurance and direction, offers experiences into areas of strength for the bonds that add to the endurance of the youthful. Preservation methodologies that focus on the insurance of the two grown-ups and their posterity are critical for the supported development of rhinoceros populaces.

Dangers to Rhinoceros Life systems

As we wonder about the complexities of rhinoceros life systems, it is fundamental to recognize the approaching dangers that imperil their reality. From poaching and environment misfortune to the difficulties presented by human-natural life clashes, the rhinoceros family faces a heap of difficulties that request earnest consideration and purposeful protection endeavors.

Poaching and Its Effect on Horn and Conceal Protection

Poaching stays a grave danger to rhinoceros populaces, driven principally by the interest for their horns in unlawful business sectors. The heartless quest for these magnificent animals for their horns jeopardizes individual lives as well as upsets the sensitive equilibrium of biological systems. Preservation drives should address the main drivers of poaching while at the same time executing successful measures to safeguard rhinoceros life structures.

Environment Misfortune and Its Impacts on Rhinoceros Populaces

As human populaces extend and scenes change, rhinoceroses are gone up against with the deficiency of their regular living spaces. Deforestation, rural extension, and urbanization add to territory fracture, segregating rhinoceros populaces and restricting their admittance to assets. Protection methodologies should address these territory related difficulties to guarantee the all around was of rhinoceroses.

Preservation Endeavors and Drives

Notwithstanding raising dangers, various protection endeavors and drives endeavor to defend the eventual fate of the rhinoceros family. Cooperative undertakings between state run administrations, non-legislative associations, and neighborhood networks center around hostile to poaching measures, environment security, and local area schooling. Looking at these protection drives offers expect the conservation of rhinoceros life structures and biodiversity at large.

Logical Exploration and Mechanical Progressions

Logical examination assumes a significant part in unwinding the secrets of rhinoceros life systems and conduct. Progressions in innovation give significant devices to scientists, empowering non-meddlesome perception and information assortment. From hereditary investigations to satellite following, the mix of logical examination and innovation improves how we might interpret rhinoceros species and illuminates preservation methodologies.

Job of Exploration in Figuring out Rhinoceros Life structures

Logical exploration contributes essentially to how we might interpret rhinoceros life systems, conduct, and environmental jobs. Through physical examinations, analysts gain bits of knowledge into the physiological variations that empower rhinoceroses to flourish in assorted conditions. This information frames the reason for informed protection choices that address the particular necessities of every species.

Mechanical Apparatuses Involved in Concentrating on Rhinoceros Species

Mechanical progressions offer a set-up of devices for concentrating on rhinoceros species without unduly upsetting their normal ways of behaving. GPS following, camera traps, and remote detecting advances give analysts uncommon admittance to the existences of these tricky animals. The joining of these instruments improves our capacity to screen populaces, distinguish dangers, and carry out designated protection intercessions.

Late Revelations and Progressions in Rhinoceros Science

The unique field of rhinoceros science ceaselessly yields new disclosures and progressions. From leap forwards in regenerative advances to bits of knowledge into their social designs, late exploration adds to our developing comprehension of rhinoceros species. Keeping up to date with these revelations is fundamental for molding preservation methodologies that adjust to arising difficulties.

1.1 Taxonomy and classification

Scientific categorization and grouping act as the key parts of how we might interpret biodiversity, giving a precise structure that sorts out the immense range of living organic entities on The planet. This perplexing field of study names and arranges species as well as unwinds the transformative connections among them. In this thorough investigation, we dig into the significant domains of scientific categorization and grouping, analyzing their authentic establishments, contemporary strategies, and the crucial job they play in explaining the embroidery of life.

Verifiable Groundworks of Scientific categorization

The foundations of scientific classification can be followed back to antiquated civic establishments where people initially perceived the need to sort out and name the residing scene around them. Notwithstanding, it was the Swedish naturalist Carl Linnaeus in the eighteenth century who laid the preparation for the cutting edge arrangement of scientific categorization. Linnaeus presented the binomial classification, a normalized naming framework where every species is distinguished by a two-section Latin name, comprising of its family and species. This progressive framework gave a generally perceived language to researchers to convey about living life forms.

The Significance of Scientific classification

Scientific categorization fills a bunch of needs, reaching out a long ways past the simple demonstration of naming species. At its center, scientific categorization is fundamental for understanding and listing biodiversity, an essential for protection endeavors and natural examination. By giving a methodical design, scientific classification permits researchers to order life forms in light of shared qualities, opening experiences into their developmental narratives and environmental jobs.

Standards of Grouping

The characterization of organic entities is directed by a bunch of rules that think about their transformative connections and shared qualities. These standards incorporate morphology (actual characteristics), hereditary qualities, conduct, and environmental specialties. A very much planned order framework expects to mirror the normal connections among organic entities, uncovering a progressive design from more extensive classes to additional particular ones.

Ordered Positions

The progressive construction of scientific classification contains different positions, each indicating a degree of association. These positions, from wide to explicit, incorporate area, realm, phylum, class, request, family, sort, and species. As life forms are grouped, they are relegated to these positions in light of their common attributes and transformative connections. For instance, people have a place with the space Eukarya, the realm Animalia, the phylum Chordata, the class Mammalia, the request Primates, the family Hominidae, the sort Homo, and the species sapiens.

Present day Ordered Apparatuses and Methods

Headways in innovation have altered the field of scientific categorization, furnishing researchers with amazing assets to unwind the intricacies of the regular world. DNA sequencing, specifically, has turned into a foundation of present day scientific classification. The investigation of hereditary material permits researchers to dive into the sub-atomic marks that support transformative connections, frequently prompting amendments and refinements of arrangements.

DNA Barcoding

DNA barcoding is a particular method that includes sequencing a short, normalized fragment of an organic entity's DNA to recognize and recognize species. This technique has demonstrated priceless in situations where morphological qualities alone might be lacking for precise distinguishing proof. DNA barcoding has applications in different fields, from biodiversity evaluations to legal examinations.

Phylogenetics

Phylogenetics is the investigation of transformative connections among organic entities, frequently addressed through phylogenetic trees. These trees portray the spreading examples of shared family line and give a visual portrayal of how species are connected. Sub-atomic information, for example, DNA successions, are normally utilized in phylogenetic examinations to develop exact and point by point trees that enlighten the transformative history of various taxa.

Scientific classification in the Time of Genomics

The coming of genomics, the investigation of a creature's whole hereditary material, has introduced another time for scientific classification. Genomic information offer extraordinary bits of knowledge into the hereditary cosmetics of life forms, permitting researchers to investigate their developmental connections as well as the useful meaning of explicit qualities. As innovations keep on propelling, genomics holds the possibility to reclassify how we might interpret biodiversity and species connections.

Difficulties and Debates in Scientific classification

While scientific categorization has significantly progressed how we might interpret the regular world, it isn't without difficulties and debates. Species delimitation, the most common way of characterizing what comprises an animal varieties, can be disagreeable, particularly in situations where organic entities show critical variety inside populaces. Moreover, the revelation of mysterious species — species that seem indistinguishable yet are hereditarily particular — presents difficulties to customary ordered strategies.

The Job of Resident Science in Scientific categorization

Lately, resident science drives play had a pivotal impact in extending the scope of scientific classification. Stages, for example, iNaturalist and eBird permit people to contribute perceptions of plants, creatures, and organisms, giving an abundance of information to ordered research. Resident researchers add to species ID, dispersion planning, and, surprisingly, the revelation of new species, featuring the democratization of logical information.

Uses of Scientific categorization Past Arrangement

Scientific categorization expands its impact a long ways past the domain of order. Its applications pervade assorted logical disciplines and useful fields, adding to agribusiness, medication, protection, and, surprisingly, criminological examinations. Understanding the connections between organic entities supports the advancement of drugs, the administration of intrusive species, and the protection of imperiled environments.

Preservation Ramifications of Scientific classification

Scientific categorization is indistinguishable from protection science, as precise species ID is crucial to viable preservation methodologies. The Worldwide Association for Protection of Nature (IUCN) Red Rundown depends on ordered evaluations to sort the preservation status of species, giving a basic instrument to focusing on preservation endeavors. Moreover, scientific classification illuminates environment rebuilding projects by distinguishing key species connections and biological jobs.

Future Bearings in Scientific categorization

As innovative headways keep on reshaping the logical scene, the eventual fate of scientific classification holds energizing prospects. Coordinating multi-disciplinary methodologies, including genomics, biology, and man-made consciousness, will refine how we might interpret species connections and rethink the models for order. The continuous investigation of microbial variety, frequently disregarded in conventional scientific categorization, is supposed to yield momentous disclosures.

1.2 Evolutionary history

The developmental history of life on Earth is a story of striking changes, traversing billions of years and leading to the stunning variety of living beings that occupy our planet today. This excursion through time uncovers the complex dance of variation, eradication, and advancement that has impacted life at its center.

Starting points of Life

The story starts in the early stage soup of Earth's initial seas, where the primary stirrings of life arose. While the subtleties of life's beginnings remain covered in secret, it is broadly acknowledged that straightforward natural particles progressively gathered, shaping the structure blocks of additional perplexing designs. Over ages, these early living things developed and expanded, making way for the horde types of life we notice today.

The Ascent of Prokaryotes: Earth's Most memorable Occupants

Among the earliest living things were prokaryotes, straightforward single-celled organic entities coming up short on a core. Microscopic organisms and archaea, the two essential parts of prokaryotic life, ruled the Earth for the initial not many billion years. These microorganisms assumed a significant part in forming the planet's air through cycles like photosynthesis, step by step changing it into a climate more helpful for life.

Eukaryotes: The Development of Intricate Cells

A crucial crossroads in developmental history happened with the coming of eukaryotes, cells with particular cores and organelles encased in layers. The combination of less complex prokaryotic cells probably brought about these more perplexing designs. The rise of eukaryotes prepared for the development of multicellular living beings, denoting a significant change in the intricacy and association of life.

The Cambrian Blast: An Eruption of Biodiversity

Around a long time back, during the Cambrian time frame, Earth saw a blast of biodiversity known as the Cambrian Blast. During this moderately short land period, the variety of life on Earth quickly expanded, with the development of perplexing marine organic entities showing a wide cluster of body plans. This occasion established the groundwork for the improvement of different phyla and set up for the advancement of more unpredictable living things.

The Time of Fishes: Development of Vertebrates

The expanses of the Silurian and Devonian periods saw the advancement of jawed fishes, denoting the appearance of vertebrates. These early fishes showed an exceptional variety of structures, adjusting to different biological specialties. Over the long run, vertebrates wandered onto land, starting the colonization of earthly conditions — a developmental jump that would shape the course of life on The planet.

Creatures of land and water, Reptiles, and the Triumph of Land

The progress from oceanic to earthly life finished in the advancement of creatures of land and water, the main vertebrates to possess both land and water. This prepared for the rise of reptiles, which, outfitted with amniotic eggs, had the option to duplicate ashore without the requirement for an oceanic climate. Reptiles, including dinosaurs, thrived during the Mesozoic Period, ruling earthbound biological systems for a long period of time.

Mass Eliminations and the Ascent of Vertebrates

Over Earth's time, mass terminations play had a pivotal impact in reshaping the direction of development. The most popular of these occasions happened around quite a while back, denoting the conclusion of the Mesozoic Age. The effect of a space rock or comet, joined with volcanic action, prompted the elimination of the dinosaurs. This disastrous occasion set out natural open doors for warm blooded animals, which quickly broadened and filled empty specialties. The ascent of well evolved creatures laid the foundation for the possible development of people.

Primates and the Development of Knowledge

The development of primates, a different request of warm blooded creatures that incorporates lemurs, monkeys, and gorillas, addresses a critical section in the narrative of life's intricacy. Primates, recognized by their getting a handle on hands, front oriented eyes, and enormous minds, developed to explore the complicated conditions of trees. After some time, certain primate genealogies, including hominins, showed an expansion in mind size and mental capacities.

Hominin Development: The Way to Humankind

The hominin ancestry, which incorporates people and our nearest family members, went through huge developmental changes over the beyond barely any million years. From early hominins like Australopithecus to the variety Homo, described by bigger cerebrum sizes and the utilization of apparatuses, the account of hominin advancement is set apart by versatility, advancement, and the improvement of social ways of behaving. The rise of Homo sapiens, physically current people, happened about quite a while back.

Social Development: A Special Human Direction

While organic development molded the actual properties of people, social advancement turned into a characterizing element of our species. The advancement of language, complex social orders, and mechanical developments sped up the speed of progress in human societies. This remarkable type of advancement permitted people to adjust to different conditions and change the direction of their own turn of events.

Contemporary Advancement and the Anthropocene

In the current time, mankind winds up at the very front of an age named the Anthropocene, described by the huge effect of human exercises in the world. The developmental direction of numerous species, including our own, is currently laced with human-actuated changes to the climate. As we wrestle with issues, for example, environmental change, biodiversity misfortune, and biological disturbance, the narrative of developmental history takes on new aspects, featuring the interconnectedness of all life on The planet.

1.3 Geographic distribution of rhinoceros species

The rhinoceros, a charming and notorious animal types, is disseminated across different mainlands, adjusting to a scope of biological systems and environments. Understanding the geographic circulation of rhinoceros species is essential for both valuing their biological jobs and carrying out compelling protection systems. This investigation takes us on an excursion across mainlands, divulging the different scenes that these glorious animals call home.

African Rhinoceros Species: White and Dark Rhinoceros

The African mainland is home to two types of rhinoceros: the White Rhinoceros (Ceratotherium simum) and the Dark Rhinoceros (Diceros bicornis). The White Rhinoceros, including the Southern White Rhinoceros and the basically jeopardized Northern White Rhinoceros, essentially possesses fields and savannas of southern Africa. Their geographic reach stretches out from South Africa to Namibia, Zimbabwe, and Kenya. The Dark Rhinoceros, recognized by its snared upper lip, flourishes in a more extensive scope of territories, including meadows, savannas, and woodlands, and is disseminated across different nations in sub-Saharan Africa.

Asian Rhinoceros Species: Indian, Javan, and Sumatran Rhinoceros

In Asia, three rhinoceros species have cut out specialties in assorted scenes. The Indian Rhinoceros (Rhinoceros unicornis) is local to the Indian subcontinent, especially tracked down in the meadows and bogs of Nepal, India, and Bhutan. With a solitary horn trademark, the Indian Rhinoceros is a demonstration of the flexibility of these animals in the changed environments of South Asia.

The Javan Rhinoceros (Rhinoceros sondaicus) is a really uncommon species, with its dissemination restricted to explicit districts in Java, Indonesia. As quite possibly of the most basically imperiled enormous vertebrate, the Javan Rhinoceros faces the danger of termination because of environment misfortune and human infringement.

The Sumatran Rhinoceros (Dicerorhinus sumatrensis) finishes the threesome of Asian rhinoceros species, possessing disconnected pockets in Sumatra and Borneo. This species is additionally under serious danger, with little divided populaces battling against the tensions of natural surroundings misfortune and poaching.

Developmental History and Biogeography

The appropriation of rhinoceros species mirrors their developmental history and the verifiable changes in Earth's topography. Fossil proof recommends that rhinoceroses once wandered across a greater reach, remembering districts for Europe, North America, and Asia. In any case, changes in environment and natural circumstances, combined with the impact of human exercises, have added to the ongoing appropriation designs noticed.

The topographical disconnection of rhinoceros populaces has impacted the improvement of particular species and subspecies. The developmental excursion of rhinoceroses has been formed by their capacity to adjust to various biological specialties, bringing about the different cluster of species we see today.

African Rhino Environments: Savannas and Prairies

The African rhinoceros species, both White and Dark Rhinoceros, transcendently possess savannas and prairies. These broad scenes offer a blend of open spaces and vegetation, giving adequate brushing potential open doors to these herbivores. The White Rhinoceros, specifically, is very much adjusted to the verdant fields, using its wide, square-formed mouth to nibble on bountiful vegetation.

Savannas are dynamic biological systems with a blend of grasses and dispersed trees, establishing a climate that upholds an assortment of untamed life. The rhinoceros, as a cornerstone animal groups, assumes a significant part in molding these environments through its brushing exercises, impacting plant networks and working with supplement cycling.

Asian Rhino Living spaces: Prairies, Marshes, and Rainforests

The Asian rhinoceros species display a more extensive scope of environments contrasted with their African partners. The Indian Rhinoceros, with its inclination for meadows and bogs, is a trademark types of the Indian subcontinent's different scenes. Streams and wetlands assume a crucial part in the Indian Rhinoceros' environment determination, giving both food and fundamental water sources.

The Javan Rhinoceros, however basically jeopardized and restricted in dispersion, is related with thick rainforests and marshes. The difficulties looked by this species are exacerbated by the deficiency of its favored territories, as timberlands are cleared for horticultural purposes and human settlements.

The Sumatran Rhinoceros, tracked down in the lavish rainforests of Sumatra and Borneo, explores the complicated environments of Southeast Asia. These thick backwoods give a shelter to biodiversity, and the rhinoceros adds to the biological offset through its cooperations with plants and different creatures.

Factors Impacting Geographic Dispersion

The geographic circulation of rhinoceros species is impacted by a blend of biological elements, verifiable cycles, and human exercises. The accessibility of reasonable living spaces, including admittance to food, water, and reasonable favorable places, assumes a urgent part in deciding the scope of rhinoceros populaces.

Environment likewise adds to the dispersion designs, as rhinoceroses are adjusted to explicit temperature and precipitation systems. Changes in environment throughout geographical time scales have likely impacted the authentic scope of rhinoceros species.

Human exercises, especially natural surroundings obliteration and discontinuity, have become predominant variables influencing the geographic appropriation of rhinoceros populaces. Deforestation, rural extension, and urbanization have infringed upon rhinoceros territories, prompting living space misfortune and seclusion of populaces.

Protection Difficulties and Dangers

The geographic conveyance of rhinoceros species is unpredictably connected to the protection challenges they face. Regardless of their flexibility, rhinoceros populaces are presently under extreme danger, essentially because of human-incited factors.

Poaching and Unlawful Natural life Exchange

Poaching for rhinoceros horns stays one of the most squeezing dangers to their endurance. The interest for rhinoceros horns, driven by customary convictions and unlawful business sectors, has energized a worthwhile exchange. Rhinoceros horns are pursued for their alleged restorative properties and as superficial points of interest, prompting broad poaching and the unlawful exchange of rhino items.

This danger is especially articulated in African rhinoceros species, where populaces have been obliterated by poaching. Protection endeavors have increased to battle poaching through enemy of poaching watches, local area commitment, and global joint efforts to control the interest for rhino horns.

Living space Misfortune and Discontinuity

Living space misfortune, driven by horticultural extension, logging, and framework improvement, represents a critical danger to rhinoceros populaces. As their regular territories lessen, rhinoceros populaces become divided and confined, prompting decreased hereditary variety and restricting the capacity of people to track down reasonable mates.

The Javan and Sumatran Rhinoceros species, currently restricted in conveyance, face uplifted takes a chance because of territory misfortune. Deforestation and land change for palm oil estates, specifically, have been impeding to the excess living spaces of these basically imperiled species.

Environmental Change

Environmental change represents an arising danger to rhinoceros territories. Changes in temperature and precipitation designs, alongside outrageous climate occasions, can affect the accessibility of water and reasonable vegetation. Environment prompted changes in natural surroundings sythesis may likewise influence the circulation of plant species that rhinoceroses depend on for food.

Preservation techniques should consider the expected effects of environmental change on rhinoceros territories, requiring versatile measures to alleviate these impacts.

Human-Untamed life Struggle

As human populaces grow and infringe upon regular environments, clashes among people and rhinoceroses can heighten. Crop striking by rhinoceroses, especially in regions where agribusiness is infringing into their natural surroundings, can prompt counter by ranchers. Tending to human-natural life struggle requires cooperative endeavors that balance the necessities of nearby networks with the protection of rhinoceros populaces.

Protection Drives and Examples of overcoming adversity

Regardless of the impressive difficulties, various preservation drives have been executed to shield rhinoceros species and their environments. Preservation associations, legislative organizations, and neighborhood networks team up to address poaching, natural surroundings misfortune, and different dangers. Fruitful preservation stories highlight the strength of rhinoceros populaces when given sufficient security and the executives.

Against Poaching Endeavors

Hostile to poaching measures, including expanded watching, the utilization of innovation like robots and infrared cameras, and the arrangement of prepared work force, have been instrumental in checking poaching exercises. The devotion of officers and preservationists on the ground assumes a basic part in shielding rhinoceros populaces from the tenacious danger of unlawful hunting.

Local area Based Protection

Drawing in neighborhood networks in preservation endeavors is urgent for the drawn out progress of rhinoceros protection. Local area put together drives center with respect to bringing issues to light, giving elective vocations, and including nearby occupants in the assurance of rhinoceros natural surroundings. By adjusting preservation objectives to the requirements and goals of nearby networks, these drives make a common obligation to saving rhinoceros species.

Movement and Renewed introduction Projects

Movement and renewed introduction programs have been carried out to lay out or reinforce rhinoceros populaces in regions where they were once extirpated or to increment hereditary variety. These projects include cautiously moving rhinoceros people to appropriate living spaces, frequently in safeguarded holds. Fruitful renewed introduction endeavors have added to the recuperation of some rhinoceros populaces.

Global Joint effort and Regulation

Worldwide joint effort is fundamental for tending to the worldwide difficulties confronting rhinoceros species. Arrangements, for example, the Show on Global Exchange Jeopardized Types of Wild Fauna and Greenery (Refers to) direct the worldwide exchange of rhinoceros items and give a system to facilitated protection endeavors. Solid regulation, both at public and global levels, goes about as an impediment to poaching and unlawful exchange.

Future Possibilities and Difficulties

The eventual fate of rhinoceros species relies on supported preservation endeavors, creative methodologies, and worldwide collaboration. While certain populaces have given indications of recuperation, challenges endure, and new dangers keep on arising.

Mechanical Advancements in Protection

Headways in innovation, like satellite following, hereditary observing, and man-made consciousness, offer promising devices for rhinoceros protection. Satellite following permits constant checking of rhinoceros developments, helping with hostile to poaching endeavors. Hereditary checking surveys the wellbeing and hereditary variety of populaces, illuminating rearing and renewed introduction programs.

Man-made reasoning is progressively being utilized for prescient displaying of poaching exercises and breaking down enormous datasets to distinguish patterns and examples. The mix of these innovative apparatuses upgrades the accuracy and effectiveness of protection drives.

Tending to Underlying drivers of Poaching

To battle poaching actually, it is vital for address the underlying drivers that drive interest for rhinoceros horns. This includes drawing in with nearby networks, bringing issues to light about the natural significance of rhinoceroses, and supporting maintainable vocations that decrease reliance on criminal operations. Global missions to expose legends encompassing the restorative properties of rhino horns and abatement the interest for these items are additionally necessary to protection endeavors.

Environment Versatile Protection Techniques

Given the vulnerabilities related with environmental change, preservation systems should integrate strength and versatility. This might include establishing environment versatile passageways to work with the development of rhinoceros populaces because of changing natural circumstances. Observing and demonstrating environment influences on rhinoceros living spaces will be vital for informed dynamic in preservation arranging.

Adjusting Preservation and Advancement

Tending to the complicated difficulties looked by rhinoceros populaces requires a fragile harmony between protection objectives and human turn of events. Supportable improvement rehearses that focus on biodiversity protection, natural surroundings safeguarding, and local area prosperity can make an amicable conjunction among people and rhinoceroses. Incorporating protection into more extensive improvement systems guarantees the drawn out practicality of rhinoceros populaces.

Chapter 2

Morphology And Physical Characteristics

Morphology, the investigation of the structure and construction of creatures, gives a passage to figuring out the complexities of life's actual qualities. From the littlest microorganisms to the most superb warm blooded creatures, the different morphologies across the tree of life serve both stylish and versatile capabilities. This investigation dives into the universe of morphology, disentangling the entrancing actual highlights that characterize and empower the horde types of life on The planet.

Characterizing Morphology in the Natural Setting

In the natural domain, morphology envelops the investigation of an organic entity's outer and interior designs. This multidisciplinary field looks at the shapes, sizes, and plans of cells, tissues, and organs, revealing insight into the transformative and practical parts of living creatures. Morphological elements incorporate everything from the moment subtleties of cell designs to the overall body plans of various species.

Cell Morphology: The Groundwork of Life

At the minute level, cell morphology frames the underpinning of life. The different shapes and designs of cells are adjusted to their particular capabilities. For example, the prolonged state of muscle cells considers contractile developments, while the complex fanning of neurons works with correspondence inside the sensory system. Cell morphology not just mirrors the hereditary data encoded in an organic entity's DNA yet additionally impacts its physiological abilities.

Tissues and Organs: Building Blocks of Intricacy

The association of cells into endlessly tissues into organs adds to the intricacy of morphological designs in multicellular organic entities. Each tissue type — epithelial, connective, muscle, and anxious — fills a particular need, and their plan characterizes the general design of organs. From the pulsating heart to the separating kidneys, the variety of organ morphology lines up with explicit physiological capabilities fundamental for a living being's endurance.

Variations in Plant Morphology: Structure and Capability in Verdure

Plants show a bewildering cluster of morphological variations that empower them to flourish in different conditions. The investigation of plant morphology incorporates elements, for example, leaf shapes, stem designs, and underground roots, each custom-made to address explicit environmental difficulties.

Leaf Morphology: The changed states of leaves, from the needle-like designs of conifers to the wide, level leaves of deciduous trees, are variations to improve photosynthesis, water maintenance, and temperature guideline. Leaf structures, for example, stomata and trichomes, further add to these variations.

Stem Morphology: The assorted types of stems, including herbaceous and woody designs, direct the plant's development propensity, water capacity limit, and mechanical help. Stems additionally act as conductors for the transportation of water, supplements, and sugars all through the plant.

Root Morphology: Root foundations, going from stringy to taproot structures, are fundamental for securing plants in the dirt and working with supplement take-up. Extrinsic roots, emerging from non-root tissues, offer extra help and help in supplement retention.

Regenerative Morphology: Blossoms, organic products, and seeds address basic parts of plant conceptive morphology. The shapes, sizes, and designs of these conceptive organs add to the outcome of plant proliferation, working with fertilization, seed dispersal, and the foundation of new ages.

Creature Morphology: Variety in Transformation

Creatures grandstand an amazing variety of morphological transformations that empower them to explore and flourish in their particular surroundings. From the smoothed out groups of fish to the strong appendages of earthbound well evolved creatures, these variations mirror the mind boggling interchange among structure and capability.

Avian Morphology: Birds, adjusted for flight, display specific morphological highlights. Their lightweight bones, fall molded sternum for muscle connection, and productive respiratory frameworks add to their ethereal ability. Snout morphology shifts broadly, reflecting variations to various weight control plans, from the examining mouths of hummingbirds to the strong bills of raptors.

Mammalian Morphology: Warm blooded creatures, an exceptionally different class of vertebrates, feature a variety of morphological variations. Appendage morphology differs as indicated by the method of headway — whether adjusted for running, swimming, climbing, or flying. Dentition, custom fitted to dietary inclinations, goes from the sharp flesh eating teeth of hunters to the crushing molars of herbivores.

Marine Warm blooded animals: Variations in marine vertebrates represent how morphology can develop to address the difficulties of sea-going life. Smoothed out bodies, flippers, and fat layers in cetaceans improve lightness and hydrodynamics. Pinnipeds, like seals and ocean lions, have appendages changed into flippers for proficient swimming.

Bug Morphology: Bugs, the most various gathering of creatures on The planet, show exceptional morphological variety. Their exoskeletons, sectioned bodies, and concentrated limbs add to their outcome in different biological specialties. Transformations like wings, recieving wires, and mouthparts mirror the assorted ways of life and taking care of propensities for various bug species.

Human Morphology: Physical Miracles of Homo sapiens

Human morphology is portrayed by an interesting arrangement of variations that recognize Homo sapiens from different species. Bipedalism, an upstanding position and stride, is a characterizing element of human morphology, liberating the hands for instrument use and working with really long travel. The opposable thumb and accuracy grasp improve aptitude, empowering the control of articles and toolmaking.

Cranial morphology in people obliges the improvement of a huge, complex mind — the seat of cognizance, language, and critical thinking. The exceptional construction of the human pelvis reflects transformations for bipedal velocity and the difficulties of labor.

While people share a typical physical outline, individual and populace level varieties in morphology are impacted by hereditary elements, ecological circumstances, and social practices. These varieties add to the rich embroidery of human variety saw across various populaces.

Morphological Variations in Outrageous Conditions

Life has figured out how to flourish in probably the cruelest and most outrageous conditions on The planet. The morphological variations of creatures in outrageous circumstances exhibit the strength and resourcefulness of life.

Extremophiles: Microorganisms known as extremophiles possess conditions with outrageous circumstances, like high temperatures, corrosiveness, or saltiness. Their morphological transformations incorporate novel film designs, proteins, and defensive systems that permit them to get by and thrive in conditions once thought cold.

Desert Transformations: Plants and creatures in desert conditions display morphological elements that assist them with adapting to dry circumstances. Delicious plants store water in plump tissues, while creatures like camels have specific transformations, including bumps for water capacity and proficient thermoregulation components.

Icy and Antarctic Transformations: Species in polar areas exhibit morphological variations for endurance in outrageous virus. Thick fur, lard layers, and minimized body structures assist warm blooded creatures with loving polar bears and seals hold heat. In the mean time, birds like penguins have smoothed out bodies and flipper-like wings for productive swimming.

Mimicry and Cover: Morphological Procedures for Endurance

Mimicry and cover are morphological procedures utilized by life forms to sidestep hunters or upgrade their hunting abilities. These transformations include the similarity of a life form to its environmental factors or to another organic entity, giving an endurance advantage.

Batesian Mimicry: In Batesian mimicry, innocuous or consumable species advance to look like poisonous or destructive species, acquiring assurance from hunters. For instance, a few non-venomous snakes copy the hue and examples of venomous snakes, deflecting likely hunters.

Müllerian Mimicry: Müllerian mimicry includes at least two unsafe or unpalatable species developing to look like one another. This mutualistic mimicry improves the general viability of caution signals, as hunters figure out how to keep away from any living being with a common appearance.

Cover: Disguise is an inescapable morphological variation where a creature's tinge and examples match its environmental factors, delivering it subtle. Models incorporate stick bugs looking like twigs, peppered moths mixing into tree rind, and hunters like chameleons changing variety to match their current circumstance.

Morphological Development: A Window into Transformative Narratives

The investigation of morphology fills in as a window into the developmental chronicles of species. Near morphology, the assessment of physical likenesses and contrasts among organic entities, gives bits of knowledge into shared family line and transformative connections.

Homologous Designs: Homologous designs are morphological elements that share a typical developmental beginning, regardless of whether they serve various capabilities. The pentadactyl appendage, with a comparative plan of bones in the appendages of vertebrates, reptiles, and birds, is an exemplary illustration of homologous designs showing a common lineage.

Undifferentiated from Designs: Closely resembling structures are morphological elements that have comparative capabilities however unique transformative starting points. Wings in bats and birds address an illustration of united advancement, where particular heredities develop comparative variations in light of comparable ecological difficulties.

Minimal Designs: Minimal designs are leftovers of organs or designs that played a practical part in the developmental precursors of an animal varieties yet have lost their unique capability over the long run. The human reference section and the wings of flightless birds are instances of minimal designs.

Morphology in Scientific categorization: Arranging Life's Variety

The field of scientific classification depends intensely on morphological qualities for arranging and distinguishing organic entities. Taxonomists utilize a mix of outside and inside morphological highlights to bunch organic entities into progressive classes in light of their transformative connections.

Ordered Positions: Ordered positions, including space, realm, phylum, class, request, family, variety, and species, are alloted in light of shared morphological attributes. Morphological qualities like the presence of wings, the design of conceptive organs, and skeletal highlights are basic in the grouping system.

Phylogenetics: Phylogenetic investigation, which thinks about both morphological and sub-atomic information, remakes the transformative connections among species. Morphological characters, whether morphometric estimations or physical highlights, add to the development of phylogenetic trees that portray the fanning examples of transformative heredities.

Human Effect on Morphology: Developmental Reactions to Anthropogenic Tensions

The impact of human exercises on the climate has prompted quick changes in the morphologies of certain species. Anthropogenic tensions, including environment modification, contamination, and environmental change, drive versatile reactions in specific populaces.

Metropolitan Advancement: A few animal categories have displayed morphological variations because of urbanization. Metropolitan dwelling birds, for instance, may foster more limited wings and snouts, permitting them to move in restricted spaces and take advantage of new food sources.

Modern Melanism: The peculiarity of modern melanism in moths addresses a striking illustration of morphological development driven by human-prompted natural changes. Peppered moths with dim hue became predominant in modern regions with sediment covered trees, giving disguise against hunters.

Environment Initiated Changes: Environmental change can impact the morphology of species as they adjust to moving natural circumstances. Changes in body size, phenology, and physiological qualities might happen in light of temperature varieties and modified biological elements.

2.1 General body structure

The general body design of living creatures is a demonstration of the wonderful variety and flexibility of life on The planet. From minuscule microorganisms to transcending sequoia trees, the bunch structures and elements of body structures are formed by transformative cycles and biological communications. This investigation digs into the essential rules that oversee general body structures across various realms of life, featuring the multifaceted plans that empower organic entities to flourish in their separate surroundings.

Cell Premise of Body Design: Building Blocks of Life

At the center of all living creatures lies the cell, the major unit of life. Cell association frames the premise of body structure, with cells showing an exceptional variety of shapes and works. Prokaryotic cells, coming up short on a characterized core, are exemplified by microorganisms, while eukaryotic cells, with an unmistakable core and organelles, describe plants, creatures, growths, and protists.

The specialization of cells into various kinds adds to the intricacy of body structures. Muscle cells contract for development, nerve cells communicate signals, epithelial cells structure defensive layers, and connective tissue cells offer underlying help.

The aggregate activities of these assorted cell types organize the working of tissues, organs, and frameworks inside a creature.

Tissue Association: Congruity in Variety

Tissues, totals of comparative cells cooperating, address a higher degree of association in the body. Four essential sorts of tissues — epithelial, connective, muscle, and anxious — join to shape the mind boggling engineering of organs and designs.

Epithelial Tissue: Covering body surfaces and coating interior depressions, epithelial tissue goes about as a defensive hindrance. Skin, the furthest layer of the body, is essentially made out of epithelial cells that safeguard against outside dangers. The epithelium additionally lines the intestinal system, respiratory entries, and veins, adding to specific penetrability and discharge.

Connective Tissue: Offering help, restricting, and security, connective tissue is assorted and incorporates bone, ligament, blood, and fat tissue. Collagen strands, versatile filaments, and ground substance add to the shifted properties of connective tissues. Bones, for example, act as an underlying structure, while blood capabilities in transportation and safe guard.

Muscle Tissue: Liable for development and power age, muscle tissue comes in three structures: skeletal, smooth, and cardiovascular. Skeletal muscles, appended to bones, work with willful developments, while smooth muscles control compulsory capabilities like processing. The heart's solid walls comprise of cardiovascular muscle, guaranteeing the cadenced siphoning of blood.

Sensory Tissue: Sensory tissue, contained neurons and glial cells, coordinates correspondence inside the body. Neurons send electrical signs, empowering quick correspondence, while glial cells support and safeguard neurons. The mind and spinal rope, indispensable parts of the sensory system, exhibit the complicated course of action of sensory tissue.

Organ Frameworks: Cooperative Ensemble of Capability

The mix of tissues into organs and organs into frameworks denotes the intricacy of body structures in multicellular organic entities. Every organ framework carries out unambiguous roles, adding to the general prosperity and endurance of the creature.

Integumentary Framework: The integumentary framework, involving the skin, hair, and nails, fills in as a defensive boundary against microbes, lack of hydration, and unsafe UV radiation. Sweat organs and hair follicles are essential parts, directing temperature and giving tactile criticism.

Skeletal Framework: The skeletal framework offers underlying help, insurance for inner organs, and fills in as a repository for minerals. Bones, associated by joints, empower development and keep up with the body's shape. The marrow inside bones assumes a significant part in platelet creation.

Solid Framework: Muscles, the effectors of development, are the essential parts of the strong framework. Skeletal muscles, constrained by the sensory system, contract and unwind to deliver deliberate developments. Smooth muscles, tracked down in inward organs, and cardiovascular muscles in the heart add to compulsory capabilities.

Sensory system: The sensory system, containing the cerebrum, spinal rope, and nerves, arranges reactions to boosts and controls normalphysical processes. Tangible neurons send signals from the climate, engine neurons pass orders on to muscles and organs, and interneurons process data inside the focal sensory system.

Cardiovascular Framework: The cardiovascular framework, comprising of the heart and veins, works with the course of blood all through the body. Supply routes divert oxygenated blood from the heart, while veins return deoxygenated blood. Vessels, the littlest veins, empower supplement and gas trade at the cell level.

Respiratory Framework: The respiratory framework, including the lungs and aviation routes, guarantees the trading of oxygen and carbon dioxide. Breathing includes the admission of oxygen through inward breath and the ejection of carbon dioxide through exhalation. Alveoli, minuscule air sacs in the lungs, work with gas trade.

Stomach related Framework: Answerable for supplement assimilation and waste end, the stomach related framework processes food from ingestion to discharge. Organs like the stomach, liver, and small digestive system make light of imperative jobs in breaking food, separating supplements, and killing toxic material.

Excretory Framework: The excretory framework, including the kidneys, ureters, bladder, and urethra, eliminates side-effects and abundance substances from the body. Kidneys channel blood, creating pee that is moved to the bladder for capacity and possible disposal.

Endocrine Framework: The endocrine framework controls normalphysical processes through the discharge of chemicals. Organs like the pituitary, thyroid, and adrenal organs discharge chemicals that impact development, digestion, stress reaction, and regenerative cycles.

Conceptive Framework: The regenerative framework, differing between genders, guarantees the continuation of species. Male conceptive organs incorporate the testicles, creating sperm, while females have ovaries that delivery eggs. Structures like the uterus and mammary organs assume parts in development and lactation.

Safe Framework: The resistant framework protects the body against microbes and unfamiliar substances. White platelets, antibodies, and lymphoid organs team up to perceive and dispose of hurtful trespassers while keeping up with resistance to self.

Variations in Plant Body Design: Organic Wonders

Plants display a particular arrangement of variations in their body structures, taking special care of their sessile nature and dependence on photosynthesis. These transformations are outfitted towards catching daylight, trading gases, and supporting the plant's primary uprightness.

Root foundations: Root foundations anchor plants in the dirt and work with water and supplement assimilation. Stringy root foundations, described by various slender roots, are normal in grasses, while taproot frameworks, with a solitary, prevailing root, give solidness and capacity limit.

Stems and Leaves: Stems support leaves, blossoms, and natural products, filling in as channels for water and supplements. The plan and states of leaves streamline daylight catch for photosynthesis. Changes like ringlets, thistles, and delicious stems upgrade endurance in assorted conditions.

Botanical Morphology: Regenerative designs in plants feature a scope of morphologies. Blossoms, the conceptive organs, draw in pollinators through variety, fragrance, and nectar. Organic products, shaped from treated ovaries, safeguard and scatter seeds. The variety of botanical designs reflects transformations to fertilization instruments, whether by wind, bugs, birds, or warm blooded creatures.

Transformations in Creature Body Construction: Exploring Environmental Specialties

Creature body structures have developed different transformations, mirroring their biological jobs and methodologies for endurance. These transformations envelop motion, taking care of, guard, and propagation.

Appendage Morphology: Appendage structures change generally among creatures in light of their methods of headway. Quadrupeds, like vertebrates with four appendages, show assorted transformations for strolling, running, climbing, and digging. Bipedal creatures, similar to birds and people, have advanced particular appendage structures for upstanding development.

Wings and Flight Variations: Birds and bugs exhibit noteworthy transformations for flight. Wings, highlighting various shapes and courses of action of plumes, empower lift and mobility. Bugs, with exoskeletons and jointed extremities, feature assorted wing designs and flight components.

Disguise and Mimicry: Cover and mimicry are pervasive variations for keeping away from hunters or ambushing prey. Chameleons change tone to match their environmental factors, mixing flawlessly into the climate. Bugs impersonate the presence of leaves or different creatures, giving a misleading benefit.

Cautious Designs: Creatures have advanced different guarded structures for insurance. Reinforced exoskeletons in arthropods, spines and plumes in warm blooded creatures, and poisons in creatures of land and water epitomize transformations that hinder hunters. A few animal groups, similar to the porcupine, have developed specific designs for both offense and safeguard.

Specific Members: Particular limbs add to taking care of methodologies in creatures. The long neck of a giraffe empowers perusing on tall vegetation, the prolonged tongue of an insect eating animal guides in bug catch, and the channel taking care of designs of whales work with the extraction of microscopic fish.

Transformative Patterns in Body Design: Unwinding the Past

The investigation of body structure gives experiences into transformative patterns across topographical time scales. Fossil proof, similar life structures, and phylogenetic examinations add to disentangling the transformative narratives of species.

Advances in Appendage Construction: The developmental change from amphibian to earthbound conditions is reflected in appendage structures. Tetrapods, the initial four-limbed vertebrates, grandstand the improvement of appendages adjusted for strolling ashore. Fossil proof uncovers go-between structures, like Tiktaalik, showing the progressive shift from balances to appendages.

Cranial Development: Changes in cranial morphology give hints about the transformations and ways of life of terminated species. The development of jaws and teeth in vertebrates, from early jawless fish to current well evolved creatures, reflects shifts in taking care of techniques and natural specialties.

Versatile Radiation: Versatile radiation happens when a solitary familial animal varieties leads to various different genealogies, each adjusted to various biological specialties. The finches of the Galápagos Islands, with their fluctuated bill shapes adjusted to various weight control plans, represent versatile radiation driven by environmental variety.

Focalized Advancement: Concurrent development includes the autonomous improvement of comparative attributes in irrelevant genealogies because of comparative determination pressures. Wings in bats and birds, however emerging from various designs, represent merged advancement driven by the common interest for flight.

Human Body Design: Physical Wonders and Varieties

The human body, a zenith of developmental accomplishment, exhibits a bunch of physical wonders. From the mind boggling construction of the cerebrum to the unpredictable plan of the outer muscle framework, human body structure reflects variations that have empowered Homo sapiens to flourish in assorted conditions.

Cranial Limit and Cerebrum Design: The broadened cranial limit and complex construction of the human mind recognize Homo sapiens. The cerebral cortex, liable for higher mental capabilities, displays a serious level of collapsing, expanding surface region and obliging the huge brain networks related with learning, memory, and thinking.

Skeletal Variations for Bipedalism: Bipedalism, a characterizing component of people, required transformations in the skeletal framework. The S-molded arch of the spine, the construction of the pelvis, and the arrangement of the appendages add to an upstanding stance and effective strolling. These variations liberated the hands for device use and worked with the investigation of different conditions.

Opposable Thumbs and Accuracy Hold: The opposable thumb and accuracy grasp are key transformations that empower people to control objects with ability. This transformation plays had a vital impact in toolmaking, apparatus use, and the improvement of complicated advancements, adding to the outcome of Homo sapiens as an animal varieties.

Fluctuation in Human Body Design: Human populaces display changeability in body structure due to hereditary, natural, and social elements. From varieties in skin tone and hair surface to contrasts in skeletal extents, these transformations mirror the assorted conditions and specific tensions that various populaces have encountered all through mankind's set of experiences.

2.2 Limb anatomy and adaptations

The life structures of appendages across the set of all animals mirrors a different exhibit of variations, each finely tuned to the environmental requests of an animal categories' natural surroundings and way of life. From the deft wings of birds to the strong appendages of vertebrates, the investigation of appendage life structures gives significant experiences into transformative narratives, biomechanical wonders, and the manners by which creatures collaborate with their surroundings.

1. **Developmental Beginnings of Appendages: From Balances to Feet**

   The developmental progress from balances to appendages addresses a crucial crossroads throughout the entire existence of vertebrates. Fossil proof, like the disclosure of Tiktaalik, uncovers mediator frames that overcome any issues among sea-going and earthbound ways of life. Appendages developed as transformations for exploring different conditions, with tetrapods turning into the principal vertebrates to wander onto land.

2. **Near Life systems of Appendages: A Mosaic of Variety**

   The relative life systems of appendages features the two likenesses and varieties across species. The pentadactyl appendage, described by five digits, fills in as a typical plan in tetrapods. However, adjustments flourish — from the wings of bats to the flippers of whales — displaying the versatility of appendage designs to various methods of movement and environmental specialties.

3. **Avian Appendages: Wings of Flight and Dominance of the Skies**

   Birds, the bosses of the skies, show momentous transformations in their appendage life structures. Wings, containing feathers upheld by a skeletal system, empower controlled flight.

   The humerus, sweep, and ulna structure the wing's primary establishment, while the carpometacarpus and phalanges support the many-sided wing morphology urgent for lift, mobility, and supported flight.

4. **Mammalian Appendages: An Orchestra of Transformations for Different Ways of life**

   Mammalian appendage life structures features a different exhibit of variations custom fitted to different ways of life. From the running legs of cheetahs to the tunneling forelimbs of moles, appendage structures have advanced to address explicit natural difficulties. The separation among forelimbs and hindlimbs frequently reflects specific capabilities, like getting a handle on, digging, or running.

5. **Oceanic Transformations: Appendages Changed for Life in Water**
   For oceanic organic entities, appendage transformations are fundamental for effective development through water. Blades in fish and flippers in marine well evolved creatures address joined advancement, with unmistakable appendage structures adjusted to life in sea-going conditions. The smoothed out states of these appendages limit drag and augment drive, displaying the style of amphibian variation.

6. **Earthbound Variations: Appendages Designed for Land Investigation**
   Appendage transformations for earthbound life are assorted, mirroring the shifted territories and ways of life of land-abiding organic entities. Quadrupedal well evolved creatures, with appendages situated underneath the body, show steadiness and proficient weight support. Cursorial variations, found in creatures like ponies and cheetahs, enhance appendages for quick running, underscoring step length and speed.

7. **Arboreal Variations: Appendages Made for Life in the Treetops**
   Arboreal species, adjusted to life in trees, exhibit particular appendage structures. Prehensile hands and feet, with opposable digits, empower getting a handle on and climbing. Primates, epitomizing these transformations, have adaptable appendage joints areas of strength for and, working with multifaceted developments in the three-layered climate of the backwoods shelter.

8. **Bug Appendages: The Accuracy of Jointed Extremities**
   Bugs, with their exoskeletons and jointed extremities, display appendage structures intended for a horde of capabilities. Legs adjusted for strolling, hopping, digging, and, surprisingly, getting prey grandstand the flexibility of bug appendages. The division of bug appendages considers exact control, featuring the effectiveness of jointed structures in answering different biological requests.

9. **Appendage Recovery: Nature's Shocking Versatility**
   Certain living beings, outstandingly creatures of land and water like lizards, have the uncommon capacity to recover appendages. Appendage recovery includes complex cell processes, with dedifferentiated cells framing a blastema that leads to new tissues. Understanding this peculiarity holds guarantee for regenerative medication and has suggestions for the more extensive field of tissue recovery.

10. **Appendage Biomechanics: The Material science of Headway**
    The biomechanics of appendage development envelops the material science of headway, including the interaction of muscles, bones, joints, and ligaments. Step length, muscle compression, and joint points add to the proficiency of development, whether it be the bouncing jumps of a kangaroo or the spry steps of a gazelle. Biomechanical studies uncover the multifaceted systems that empower creatures to explore their surroundings.

11. **Appendage Improvement: From Incipient organism to Useful Limb**
    The improvement of appendages in undeveloped organisms follows a preserved

hereditary program, with Hox qualities assuming a vital part in determining appendage personality. Appendage buds arise and go through mind boggling designing, prompting the arrangement of bones, muscles, and connective tissues. The investigation of appendage improvement gives bits of knowledge into the sub-atomic cycles arranging the formation of practical members.

12. **Appendage Problems and Pathologies: Bits of knowledge into Wellbeing and Transformative Heritages**

The investigation of appendage issues, both innate and procured, offers bits of knowledge into both the complexities of appendage life systems and the developmental heritages held in the human genome. Conditions, for example, polydactyly and syndactyly uncover the versatility of appendage improvement, while osteoarthritis and breaks give looks into the difficulties forced by the requests of earthly headway.

13. **Appendage Variations in Human Development: From Moving to Apparatus Use**

The development of human appendages mirrors a progress from arboreal progenitors to earthbound bipeds. Bipedalism liberated the hands for device use, a characterizing component of Homo sapiens. The opposable thumb and accuracy hold empowered the making of devices, denoting an extraordinary second in human development and the rise of mechanical development.

14. **Social Meaning of Appendages: Articulations of Character and Imaginative Motivation**

Appendage adjustments, like tattoos, piercings, and body workmanship, have social importance across human social orders. These alterations act as articulations of character, social having a place, and imaginative motivation. The variety of appendage decorations mirrors the rich embroidery of human societies and the emblematic implications ascribed to body changes.

15. **Appendage Difficulties in Outrageous Conditions: Adjusting to the Unforgiving**

Living beings in outrageous conditions, from the bone chilling Cold to singing deserts, face exceptional difficulties in appendage variation. Animals like camels and polar bears grandstand appendage structures adjusted to temperature guideline and effective development in cruel circumstances. The transformations in extremophiles give a brief look into the flexibility of life in conditions once thought to be unwelcoming.

16. **Appendage Protection: Moral Contemplations and Natural Effect**

Human exercises, from deforestation to environmental change, present dangers to the living spaces and ways of life of numerous species. Protection endeavors should think about the effect of appendage transformations on the endurance of species. Moral contemplations emerge in protection works on, underscoring the need to safeguard the creatures as well as the mind boggling transformations that have developed over centuries.

2.3 Skin characteristics and coloration

The skin, a complex organ that envelopes and safeguards the collections of different living beings, fills in as a material mirroring the multifaceted embroidery of life's transformations. Skin attributes and hue, affected by hereditary qualities, climate, and developmental tensions, assume significant parts in cover, correspondence, thermo-regulation, and assurance. This investigation dives into the intriguing universe of skin, unwinding its shifted attributes and the transformative meaning of tinge across various species.

**1. Underlying Variety of Skin: Past the Surface

The underlying variety of skin reaches out past its noticeable surface, incorporating layers that satisfy unmistakable capabilities. The epidermis, furthest layer, goes about as a defensive boundary against microorganisms and ecological stressors. The dermis offers underlying help and houses tangible receptors, while the subcutaneous tissue adds to protection and energy stockpiling. The intricacy of skin structure differs across taxa, reflecting transformations to explicit natural specialties.

2. Pigmentation: The Range of Varieties

Pigmentation, the presence of shaded particles in skin cells, is a central determinant of skin hue. Melanocytes, specific cells in the epidermis, produce melanin — the essential shade liable for skin, hair, and eye tone. The dissemination and kind of melanin add to the huge swath of complexions saw in various species. From the melanin-rich skin of people to the lively tints of reptiles, pigmentation is a dynamic and developmentally saved characteristic.

3. Disguise and Obscure Shading: Mixing In to Make due

Disguise, a pivotal part of skin hue, empowers life forms to mix consistently into their environmental elements, giving an endurance advantage. In conditions going from thick backwoods to parched deserts, species have developed mysterious shading to sidestep hunters or work with trap predation. Models incorporate the complicated examples of chameleons copying foliage or the mottled hue of specific bugs looking like their living space.

4. Aposematism: Striking Tints as Advance notice Signs

As opposed to cover, a few animal categories utilize lively and obvious hue as an advance notice sign to likely hunters — a peculiarity known as aposematism. Brilliant tones frequently show harmfulness or unpalatability, filling in as a visual obstacle. Poison dart frogs, enhanced in striking shades, embody aposematism, strongly publicizing their harmful nature to would-be hunters.

5. Correspondence through Chromatophores: The Craft of Articulation

Chromatophores, particular shade containing cells found in the skin of different creatures, empower dynamic variety changes utilized in correspondence. Cephalopods, for example, octopuses and cuttlefish, have chromatophores that can quickly grow or contract, considering complicated showcases of variety and example. These showcases serve various capabilities, from flagging hostility to drawing in mates.

6. Thermoregulation: The Dance of Light and Dull

Skin hue assumes an imperative part in thermoregulation, managing internal heat level in light of ecological circumstances. Dull pigmentation assimilates more daylight and intensity, helping with heat maintenance in colder conditions. Conversely, lighter pigmentation reflects daylight, forestalling overheating in hotter environments. The different transformations in skin shading across species mirror the perplexing dance among thermoregulation and ecological requests.

7. Sexual Dimorphism: Shading as a Sign of Wellness

Sexual dimorphism, the distinctions in appearance among guys and females, frequently reaches out to skin tinge. In numerous species, guys show more dynamic or prominent varieties for of drawing in mates. The peacock's luminous plumage and the striking shades of male birds of heaven represent how hue fills in as an obvious prompt in mate determination, flagging hereditary wellness and conceptive potential.

8. Ecological Transformations: Skin Tone as a Developmental Reaction

Skin shading addresses a transformative reaction to natural variables, including daylight power and UV radiation. Close to the equator, where UV radiation is high, more obscure skin gives improved security against the unsafe impacts of inordinate UV openness. Conversely, populaces in higher scopes with lower UV radiation show lighter complexions, considering expanded combination of vitamin D because of diminished daylight.

9. Human Skin Variety: A Developmental Embroidery

Human skin hue grandstands noteworthy variety, mirroring the intricate exchange of hereditary, ecological, and verifiable variables. Melanin levels shift among populaces, with hazier skin common in locales with high UV radiation and lighter skin in regions with lower UV openness. Human skin tone is a demonstration of the continuous transformative cycles forming our species because of different conditions and specific tensions.

10. Social and Social Importance: The Crossing point of Variety and Character

Past its organic importance, skin variety conveys social and social implications, impacting impression of character, magnificence, and having a place. The idea of race, established in authentic and social builds, has been complicatedly attached to skin tone. The assorted manners by which various societies see and worth skin variety feature the intricacy of human communications and the job of variety in forming cultural standards.

11. Issues of Pigmentation: Experiences into Skin Science

Issues of pigmentation give significant experiences into the basic science of skin hue. Conditions, for example, albinism, portrayed by the shortfall of melanin, highlight the significant job of melanocytes in deciding skin, hair, and eye tone. Concentrating on these problems adds to how we might interpret the atomic systems administering pigmentation and offers likely roads for clinical exploration.

12. Natural Dangers: Tinge as a Reaction to Contamination

In metropolitan conditions, where contamination levels are high, a few animal categories display changes in skin shading as a reaction to ecological stressors. Certain creatures, like moths and reptiles, have been noticed creating more obscure shading to disguise against dirtied surfaces. These versatile reactions highlight the significant effect of human exercises on the regular world and the capacity of living beings to adjust to evolving conditions.

Chapter 3

Horns And Their Significance

Horns, noticeable and frequently grand designs enhancing the heads of different creature species, have spellbound human interest for quite a long time. A long ways past simple stylish embellishments, horns serve different and fundamental capabilities in the normal world. This investigation digs into the complexities of horns, analyzing their developmental starting points, various structures, capabilities, and the more extensive natural and social importance they hold across various taxa.

1. Transformative Beginnings of Horns: Familial Impressions in Bone

Horns, as transformative designs, follow their beginnings to familial impressions implanted in the fossil record. While the particular transformative pathways shift among taxa, horns frequently share normal lineage with hard outgrowths, for example, ossicones in giraffes, tracked down in far off family members. Understanding the developmental history of horns reveals the unique cycles that have molded these astounding designs throughout topographical time scales.

2. Horn Types and Morphologies: The Many Essences of Polish

Horns manifest in a heap of types and morphologies, mirroring the different variations of species to their environmental specialties. Bovids, for example, dairy cattle and eland, show genuine horns — super durable designs made out of bone, covered by a keratinous sheath. Conversely, deer and some gazelle species brag tusks — transitory hard designs shed and regrown every year. Rhinoceros horns, made out of keratin strands, address an unmistakable transformation, while different species, similar to the pronghorn, exhibit stretched structures.

3. Elements of Horns: More going on than might be immediately obvious

The elements of horns reach out a long ways past simple enhancements, assuming pivotal parts in the endurance, generation, and social elements of species. Cautious weaponry is an unmistakable capability, with horns filling in as impressive impediments against hunters. Intraspecific contest for mates frequently includes elaborate shows and conflicts between horned people, displaying the job of horns in sexual determination and mate fascination.

**4. Sexual Choice and Mate Fascination: Horns as Trimmings of Force

Sexual choice, a main impetus in the development of optional sexual qualities, is clear in the ornamentation and size of horns. In numerous species, guys with bigger and more great horns are leaned toward by females during mate determination. The intricate shows and fights between guys for strength highlight the meaning of horns as images of hereditary wellness and regenerative ability.

**5. Guarded Systems: Horns as Imposing Weapons

The guarded capacities of horns are noticeably shown in conflicts with hunters. Whether used to avert hunters or take part in direct battle, horns give a method for security to species powerless against predation. The horns of rhinoceroses, for example, act as integral assets for protection against possible dangers, featuring the versatile meaning of these designs in nature.

**6. Social Order and Correspondence: Horns as Friendly Images

Horns assume a crucial part in the foundation and support of social orders inside species. Predominance and accommodation are in many cases conveyed through the size, shape, and state of horns. In species like sheep, where people structure gatherings known as groups, the progressive system is apparently reflected in the conspicuousness and state of every individual's horns.

**7. Species-Explicit Transformations: Horns in Environmental Setting

The environmental setting shapes the particular transformations of horns inside various species. For instance, the twisting horns of specific pronghorn species are appropriate for exploring thick vegetation, considering proficient development through their territories. The different types of horns across taxa mirror the natural specialties and particular tensions that have affected their advancement.

**8. Social Importance: Horns in Folklore and Imagery

All through mankind's set of experiences, horns have held social importance, highlighting conspicuously in folklore, imagery, and craftsmanship. Horned divinities, for example, the horned god Dish in Greek folklore, represent richness and the untamed powers of nature. Horns have been integrated into strict iconography, addressing strength, virility, and the heavenly. Moreover, in different societies, horned creatures are worshipped images, epitomizing qualities of force, security, and profound importance.

**9. Preservation Difficulties: Dangers to Horned Species

While horns assume basic parts in the endurance and transformation of species, they likewise make specific creatures defenseless against human-driven dangers. Poaching for horns, especially on account of rhinoceroses and certain pronghorn species, presents critical preservation challenges. Endeavors to address these dangers imply a mix of hostile to poaching measures, living space preservation, and local area commitment to safeguard these radiant animals and their notable members.

10. Human Use of Horns: From Devices to Relics

People, since the beginning of time, have used creature horns for various purposes. Horns have been designed into devices, like drinking vessels and carries out for hunting and horticulture. Imaginative articulations, from unpredictable carvings to instruments like the shofar, exhibit the flexibility of horns in human societies. Be that as it may, moral contemplations emerge as the interest for horn items influences untamed life populaces.

11. Rhino Horn Exchange: A Preservation Situation

The exchange rhinoceros horns represents a huge protection quandary. In spite of global endeavors to control unlawful exchange and safeguard rhino populaces, the interest for rhino horns perseveres, driven by conventional convictions in specific societies that attribute restorative properties to the horns. Preservation techniques include severe enemy of poaching measures, local area commitment, and endeavors to move social discernments encompassing the utilization of rhino horns.

12. Horns in Fossil science: Experiences from the Fossil Record

The investigation of fossilized horns gives significant experiences into the transformative history of different species. Scientistss break down the size, shape, and construction of fossilized horns to induce data about antiquated environments, biological specialties, and transformative patterns. Fossilized horned dinosaurs, similar to Triceratops, offer looks into the variety of horned variations in ancient conditions.

3.1 Different types of rhinoceros horns

Rhinoceros horns, notorious images of the regular world, stand as magnificent designs that have captivated and baffled mankind for a really long time. These impressive extremities, contained keratin — a similar protein tracked down in human hair and nails — fluctuate fundamentally among the five existing rhinoceros species. This investigation dives into the unmistakable kinds of rhinoceros horns, disentangling their novel attributes, transformative variations, environmental jobs, and the continuous protection challenges they face.

1. White Rhinoceros (Ceratotherium simum): The Square-Mouthed Slow eater

The white rhinoceros, with its square-molded mouth adjusted for nibbling on grasses, brags two particular sorts horns. Both male and female white rhinos ordinarily have two horns, with the front horn being bigger than the back. These horns, made out of firmly pressed keratin strands, bend forward, and can arrive at lengths of more than five feet. The white rhinoceros depends on its advanced feeling of smell to explore its green living spaces, where these imposing horns serve essentially for protection against hunters and in regional debates with conspecifics.

2. Dark Rhinoceros (Diceros bicornis): Variations for Program Way of life

The dark rhinoceros, described by its sharp upper lip adjusted for perusing on bushes and trees, likewise shows two particular horns. The front horn is regularly longer and more unmistakable, arriving at lengths of up to three and a half feet, while the back horn is more modest and might be missing in certain people. Dark rhinos are known for their lone and once in a while forceful way of behaving, and their horns assume fundamental parts in protection, region stamping, and intraspecific correspondence. Sadly, dark rhinos have confronted extreme poaching pressures, prompting critical decreases in their populaces.

3. Indian Rhinoceros (Rhinoceros unicornis): A Solitary Marvel

The Indian rhinoceros, frequently alluded to as the one-horned rhinoceros, remains as a special delegate of the rhinoceros family. Consistent with its name, this species commonly has a solitary horn, albeit intermittent people with two horns have been reported. The Indian rhinoceros occupies fields and marshes in the Indian subcontinent and Southeast Asia. The solitary horn, made out of keratin, is generally more limited than those of African species, yet it stays an unmistakable element of this magnetic species.

4. Sumatran Rhinoceros (Dicerorhinus sumatrensis): The Furry Rhino

The Sumatran rhinoceros, among the most uncommon and littlest of the rhinoceros species, displays two unmistakable highlights — thick hair covering its body and two little, pointed horns. The hair is a transformation to its woodland abiding way of life, giving protection and assurance against thick vegetation. The Sumatran rhinoceros commonly has two little horns, with the front horn being longer. These horns, similar to those of other rhinoceros species, are made out of keratin and assume parts in guard, correspondence, and possibly in exploring the thick and frequently testing woodland conditions.

5. Javan Rhinoceros (Rhinoceros sondaicus): A Solitary Horn In the midst of the Mangroves

The Javan rhinoceros, the most fundamentally jeopardized of all rhinoceros species, possesses thick tropical rainforests and mangrove swamps. Like the Indian rhinoceros, the Javan rhinoceros commonly has a solitary horn, in spite of the fact that there have been verifiable records of people with two horns. The horn is generally little and might be straight or somewhat bended. Preservation endeavors for the Javan rhinoceros are concentrated because of its shaky status, with a minuscule populace persevering in a restricted reach.

6. Developmental Importance: Transformations in Horn Design

The advancement of rhinoceros horns is complicatedly attached to the biological specialties and ways of behaving of every species. The genealogical rhinoceros probably had a solitary, basic horn, and the varieties seen today have emerged through centuries of transformation. Different particular tensions, including taking care of propensities, natural surroundings types, and social designs, have impacted the size, shape, and number of horns in every species.

7. Elements of Rhinoceros Horns: Past Stylish Allure

While rhinoceros horns without a doubt add to the magnetic allure of these grand animals, their capabilities reach out a long ways past simple style. The essential jobs of rhinoceros horns incorporate protection against hunters, intraspecific correspondence, domain checking, and expected jobs in conceptive rivalry. Understanding these capabilities is urgent for valuing the biological meaning of rhinoceros horns and concocting powerful protection methodologies.

**8. Guard Against Hunters: Imposing Weapons in Nature

Rhinoceros horns act as impressive weapons in safeguard against hunters. While rhinos are by and large hearty and very much safeguarded because of their size, the horns add an additional layer of discouragement. Rhinos are known to utilize their horns against hunters like lions, and the forward looking direction of the horns considers successful protection, especially on account of the white rhinoceros, which can charge at high rates.

**9. Intraspecific Correspondence: Horns as Images of Predominance

Inside an animal types, rhinoceros horns assume vital parts in intraspecific correspondence. Pecking orders frequently structure among guys, and the size, shape, and state of horns are huge marks of a singular's status. Horn conflicts and shows are normal during connections between conspecifics, especially with regards to laying out and keeping up with social progressive systems and in contest for mates.

**10. Domain Denoting: The Specialty of Fragrance and Horns

Rhinoceroses are regional creatures, and the stamping of domains includes obvious prompts as well as olfactory signs. The position of aroma markings on vegetation, joined with the actual presence of the rhino and the conspicuous showcase of horns, effectively depicts regional limits. The rhino's special fragrance, combined with viewable prompts from the horns, imparts an unmistakable message to possible gatecrashers.

**11. Expected Jobs in Regenerative Contest: An Orchestra of Horned Showcases

Regenerative rivalry among male rhinoceroses frequently includes elaborate shows and conflicts, with horns filling in as central focuses. Bigger and more amazing horns can be demonstrative of hereditary wellness and conceptive potential. Females, thusly, may show inclinations for guys with conspicuous horns during the mating season, adding to the elements of sexual determination inside rhinoceros populaces.

**12. Protection Difficulties: The Situation of Horned Monsters

Notwithstanding the essential environmental jobs played by rhinoceros horns, these notorious designs have turned into the focal point of extreme protection challenges. The interest for rhinoceros horns in conventional medication, especially in a few Asian societies, and the unlawful exchange rhino horn items have prompted uncontrolled poaching. Preservation endeavors include hostile to poaching measures, territory insurance, local area commitment, and tending to the main drivers of interest for rhino horn items.

**13. Dehorning as a Preservation Technique: Moral Contemplations

With an end goal to control poaching, some preservation drives have investigated the disputable act of dehorning rhinoceroses. This includes eliminating or managing the horns to decrease their fairly estimated worth and limit the impetus for poaching. In any case, dehorning raises moral contemplations, as it influences the regular ways of behaving and natural jobs of rhinoceroses. Finding some kind of harmony between protection needs and moral contemplations stays a mind boggling challenge.

14. Instructive Effort: Molding Viewpoints for Preservation

Training and effort programs assume an imperative part in forming points of view and cultivating preservation endeavors. Bringing issues to light about the environmental jobs of rhinoceros horns, the outcomes of poaching, and the more extensive meaning of rationing these famous species is fundamental for gathering public help and advancing economical practices.

15. Mechanical Developments: Instruments for Preservation

Mechanical developments, going from cutting edge global positioning frameworks to ramble observation, are being utilized in rhinoceros protection. These apparatuses help in observing rhino populaces, identifying and hindering poaching exercises, and assembling information for informed preservation methodologies. The mix of innovation into preservation rehearses exhibits the flexibility of approaches pointed toward defending rhinoceros populaces and their remarkable highlights.

3.2 Growth and development of horns

The development and improvement of horns in the animals of the world collectively unfurl as a charming ensemble, each note a demonstration of the complex dance between hereditary qualities, nature, and transformative tensions. From the spiraled greatness of mountain goats to the impressive weaponry of rhinoceroses, the excursion of horn improvement winds around an account of transformation, endurance, and natural ability. This investigation digs into the nuanced processes overseeing the development and improvement of horns, inspecting the assorted pathways taken by various species and revealing insight into the transformative meaning of these famous designs.

1. Early stage Starting points: The Beginning of Horns

The early stage starting points of horns follow back to the hereditary outline encoded in the DNA of a living being. Horn improvement starts during embryogenesis, where specific cells known as mesenchymal cells separate into the forerunner structures that will ultimately lead to horns. The outflow of explicit qualities, remembering those for the fibroblast development factor (FGF) and bone morphogenetic protein (BMP) families, arranges the development of these early horn buds.

2. Early Formative Stages: The Rise of Horn Buds

As the incipient organism creates, horn buds become noticeable, denoting the beginning phases of horn arrangement. The exact timing and area of horn bud development fluctuate among species. At times, horn buds show up not long after birth, while in others, they might be available even before birth. The size and morphology of horn buds additionally contrast, mirroring the variety of horn structures across species.

3. Hereditary Guideline: The Code for Horn Development

Hereditary guideline assumes a critical part in directing the development direction of horns. The outflow of qualities engaged with bone turn of events, for example, those encoding for different development factors and flagging proteins, directs the extension and molding of horn structures.

Hereditary variety inside populaces can prompt assorted horn morphologies, adding to the wonderful cluster of shapes and sizes saw in the animals of the world collectively.

4. Hormonal Impacts: Organizing Development Examples

Chemicals employ extensive impact over the development of horns, especially during the beginning of sexual development. In numerous species, the flood of sex chemicals, like testosterone in guys, sets off the fast development and improvement of horns. Hormonal changes and communications with development chemical assume key parts in deciding the timing, size, and primary intricacy of horns, frequently lining up with the regenerative and social elements of these members.

5. Species-Explicit Examples: Horns as Extraordinary Marks

The development examples of horns are species-explicit, mirroring the natural jobs and particular tensions looked by every creature. For instance, in bovids like sheep and goats, horns frequently show a ceaseless development design all through the creature's life, with yearly additions set apart by development rings. Conversely, tusks in deer, while at first developing quickly, go through a yearly pattern of shedding and regrowth.

6. Ceaseless Development: The Steadiness of Bovid Horns

Bovid horns, found in species like sheep, goats, and dairy cattle, exhibit a particular example of ceaseless development. Dissimilar to tusks, which are shed and regrown yearly, bovid horns persevere all through a singular's life. Development rings on the horns act as a record of the creature's age, with each ring addressing an extended time of development. The size and intricacy of bovid horns frequently increment with age, filling in as signs of a singular's encounter and predominance.

7. Tusk Development: An Occasional Scene

Tusks, normal for deer species, display an extraordinary example of occasional development. Tusk advancement ordinarily starts in spring, with quick development driven by elevated degrees of testosterone. By summer, tusks arrive at their standard and are utilized for different social and conceptive capabilities, including presentations of predominance and rivalry for mates. In late pre-winter or late-fall, the prongs are shed, and the cycle starts once more.

8. Recovery and Shedding: Nature's Restoration

The capacity to recover and shed horns or prongs is an exceptional component seen in specific species. For instance, deer shed their tusks every year, just to regrow them in the accompanying season.

This cyclic recovery considers the variation of horns to changing environmental circumstances and the requests of regenerative contest. Also, a few types of rhinoceroses, similar to the dark rhinoceros, may encounter horn wear and regrowth all through their lives.

9. Asset Designation: Difficult exercise of Development

The development and improvement of horns address a unique exchange between asset distribution and biological requests. Creatures should designate assets prudently to help horn development without compromising fundamental capabilities like generation, endurance, and by and large wellness. Advancement has calibrated the harmony between horn improvement and other life-history qualities, guaranteeing that organic entities can flourish in their particular environmental specialties.

10. Sexual Dimorphism: Horns as Markers of Orientation

Sexual dimorphism, the unmistakable contrasts in appearance among guys and females, frequently stretches out to the development examples and sizes of horns. In species where guys have horns, sexual determination and rivalry for mates drive the advancement of bigger and more intricate horns in guys. Females, conversely, may display more modest or missing horns, mirroring the differential regenerative techniques took on by every orientation.

11. Social Capabilities: Horns in the Theater of Conduct

The development and presence of horns assume vital parts in the social elements of numerous species. Intraspecific cooperations, including showcases of predominance, regional debates, and conceptive rivalry, frequently include the utilization of horns. The size, shape, and state of horns become urgent viewable prompts that intervene social orders and work with correspondence among conspecifics.

12. Natural Variations: Horns as Instruments for Endurance

The development of horns is profoundly entwined with biological transformations, molding the manners by which creatures explore and make due in their territories. Horns might act as apparatuses for scavenging, guard against hunters, or weapons in intraspecific contest. The assorted exhibit of horn structures across species mirrors the complex connections among structure and capability in light of explicit environmental difficulties.

13. Protection Suggestions: Defending Horned Miracles

The development and improvement of horns are personally attached to the preservation challenges looked by numerous species. The unlawful exchange horn items, driven by social convictions and interest for elaborate things, represents a critical danger to the endurance of rhinoceroses and other horned creatures. Protection endeavors should address these dangers while likewise considering the natural jobs played by horns in keeping up with sound environments.

14. Moral Contemplations: Finding Some kind of harmony

As traditionalists wrestle with the difficulties of safeguarding horned species, moral contemplations come to the very front. Techniques, for example, dehorning, pointed toward decreasing the motivator for poaching, bring up issues about the effect on normal ways of behaving and environmental jobs. Finding some kind of harmony between protection needs and moral contemplations stays a continuous test in the mission to shield these notable animals.

15. Instruction and Effort: Cultivating Understanding for Preservation

Instructive drives and effort programs assume a vital part in cultivating understanding and backing for the protection of horned species. By bringing issues to light about the environmental meaning of horns, the outcomes of unlawful exchange, and the more extensive ramifications for biodiversity, traditionalists can revitalize public help and drive positive change.

3.3 Functionality and purpose of horns

The set of all animals brags an exhibit eminent animals decorated with horns, each pair telling a special story of variation, endurance, and natural importance. From the spiraled polish of impala horns to the impressive weaponry of rhinoceroses, horns serve multi-layered works well established in the developmental history of species. This investigation digs into the usefulness and reason for horns, disentangling the many-sided jobs these designs play in the existences of assorted living beings across various environments.

1. Cautious Arms stockpile: Horns as Imposing Weapons

One of the essential elements of horns across different species is their job as cautious weapons. The impressive appearance and strength of horns go about as hindrances against hunters, giving a method for insurance to horned creatures. In the wild, conflicts between horned people and hunters frequently include the utilization of horns as apparatuses for protection. The white rhinoceros, with its huge forward looking horn, embodies this protective methodology, involving its horn as a considerable weapon against likely dangers.

2. Intraspecific Rivalry: Engaging for Strength

Horns assume a significant part in intraspecific rivalry, especially among guys vieing for mates and laying out strength inside a social order. The size, shape, and state of horns become obvious signs that intercede associations between conspecifics. Elaborate shows, conflicts, and ritualized battle are well known signs of intraspecific contest, where the ownership of noteworthy horns can present benefits in getting mating valuable open doors and laying out regional strength.

3. Sexual Choice: Horns as Images of Hereditary Wellness

Sexual choice, a main impetus in the development of optional sexual qualities, is in many cases clear in the ornamentation and size of horns. In numerous species, females show inclinations for guys with bigger or more intricate horns, taking into account these highlights as marks of hereditary wellness and conceptive potential. The perplexing twistings of mountain goat horns or the spreading prongs of deer stand as demonstration of the job of sexual choice in molding the variety of horn structures.

4. Regional Stamping: Horns as Limits of Room

Regional way of behaving is a typical part of creature life, and horns frequently assume a part in checking and safeguarding domains. The actual presence of horned people joined with the visual showcase of horns fills in as an unmistakable sign to conspecifics, outlining regional limits. Horns might be utilized related to fragrance markings to lay out and convey responsibility for specific space, adding to the social design of a populace.

5. Correspondence and Social Progressive system: The Language of Horns

Horns act as instruments of correspondence inside gatherings, permitting people to pass on data about their status and expectations. The size and state of horns can demonstrate a singular's age, insight, and social standing. Social progressive systems inside bunches are many times outwardly reflected in the noticeable quality of horns, with predominant people regularly having bigger or all the more all around kept up with horns. The social collection related with horns, for example, head shifting and horn shows, further improves correspondence among conspecifics.

6. Asset Procurement: Horns as Scrounging Apparatuses

In certain species, horns are adjusted for asset procurement, especially with regards to searching. Animals like cows and certain pronghorn species utilize their horns to control vegetation, arriving at high branches or taking leaves from low-hanging vegetation. The underlying transformations of horns in these species mirror their biological specialty and the difficulties related with acquiring important assets from their surroundings.

7. Natural Variations: Horns in Specialty Specialization

The variety of horn structures across species reflects explicit natural variations custom-made to various conditions. For instance, the twisting horns of mountain goats are appropriate for exploring steep, rough territory, giving steadiness during gets over and plummets. Horns likewise assume a part in thermoregulation, with veins in the horn structures adding to warm trade and supporting temperature guideline in specific species.

8. Searching and Taking care of Techniques: Horns as Expansions of the Mouth

In species where horns are adjusted for searching, these designs capability as augmentations of the mouth, permitting creatures to reach and control food sources. Bovids, for example, goats and sheep, utilize their horns to handle, contort, and pull vegetation reachable. The development of horns as particular apparatuses for searching features the adaptability of these designs in working with different natural jobs.

9. Hunter Discouragement: The Visual Language of Horns

Horns act as a visual language that conveys the status and capacity of a person to guard itself against likely hunters. The simple presence of horns, combined with the readiness of horned creatures to involve them in safeguard, goes about as an obstruction to hunters. Hunters frequently survey the gamble presented by potential prey in light of the size and impressiveness of their horns, affecting the hunter's choice to participate in an assault.

10. Regenerative Contest: Horns as Instruments of Accomplishment

Regenerative contest among guys frequently includes the utilization of horns as instruments of accomplishment. Horn size, shape, and condition become vital variables in deciding the result of rivalry for mates. Guys with noteworthy horns might enjoy a cutthroat benefit in getting mating potential open doors, as females are bound to choose mates with beneficial horn qualities. This unique highlights the job of horns in the more extensive setting of regenerative accomplishment inside populaces.

11. Social Importance: Horns in Folklore and Imagery

Past their environmental capabilities, horns hold social importance in human folklore and imagery. Horned divinities, for example, the Greek god Skillet or the Celtic Cernunnos, represent richness, ferocity, and the untamed powers of nature. Horns are frequently integrated into strict iconography and creative portrayals, addressing strength, virility, and the association among mankind and the regular world. The social imagery of horns rises above their organic capabilities, featuring the profound and persevering through effect of these designs on human creative mind.

12. Preservation Difficulties: Dangers to Horned Species

While horns assume fundamental parts in the existences of horned species, they likewise open these creatures to critical preservation challenges. The interest for horn items, driven by customary convictions and the unlawful exchange untamed life, represents an immediate danger to the endurance of rhinoceroses, impala, and other horned species. Preservation endeavors should address the underlying drivers of poaching, safeguard territories, and connect with nearby networks to shield these notable animals and their particular highlights.

13. Human Usage of Horns: From Devices to Relics

Human social orders have generally used creature horns for different purposes, going from instruments to relics. Horns have been molded into executes for hunting, drinking vessels, instruments like the shofar, and decorative things. The flexibility of horns in human societies raises moral contemplations, especially with regards to protection, as the interest for horn items influences natural life populaces.

14. Rhino Horn Exchange: A Protection Quandary

The exchange rhinoceros horns addresses an intricate preservation issue. In spite of worldwide endeavors to control unlawful exchange and safeguard rhino populaces, the interest for rhino horns endures, driven by conventional convictions in specific societies that credit restorative properties to the horns. Preservation methodologies include severe enemy of poaching measures, local area commitment, and endeavors to move social discernments encompassing the utilization of rhino horns.

15. Dehorning as a Preservation System: Difficult exercise of Morals

Despite wild poaching, some preservation drives have investigated the questionable act of dehorning rhinoceroses as a methodology to decrease the motivation for unlawful exchange. Dehorning includes eliminating or managing the horns, expecting to make rhinos less alluring focuses for poachers. In any case, dehorning raises moral contemplations, as it influences the regular ways of behaving, social elements, and natural jobs of rhinoceroses. Finding some kind of harmony between protection needs and moral contemplations stays a mind boggling challenge for moderates.

**16. Mechanical Developments: Instruments for Preservation

Mechanical developments assume a significant part in current preservation endeavors pointed toward safeguarding horned species. High level global positioning frameworks, satellite innovation, and robot observation are utilized to screen and safeguard rhinoceros populaces. These devices help in recognizing and hindering poaching exercises, gathering information for informed protection methodologies, and adding to the general viability of preservation drives.

**17. Instruction and Effort: Encouraging Preservation Awareness

Instructive effort programs are fundamental for encouraging protection cognizance and accumulating public help. By bringing issues to light about the environmental elements of horns, the outcomes of poaching, and the more extensive ramifications for biodiversity, moderates can draw in networks and people in endeavors to safeguard horned species. Training assumes a significant part in forming perspectives, ways of behaving, and strategies that add to the protection of these notorious animals.

**18. Moral Contemplations in Preservation: An All encompassing Methodology

Preservation endeavors that include horned species require an all encompassing methodology that offsets natural contemplations with moral standards. Finding some kind of harmony between human necessities, social practices, and the protection of biodiversity is fundamental. Moral contemplations reach out past the immediate preservation of horned species to envelop more extensive issues of living space assurance, reasonable asset use, and the advancement of concurrence among people and natural life.

**19. Environmental Change and Living space Misfortune: Effects on Horned Species

The effects of environmental change and living space misfortune represent extra difficulties for horned species. Changes in temperature, precipitation examples, and vegetation creation can influence the accessibility of assets and modify environmental elements. Protection techniques should address the interconnected difficulties of environmental change, natural surroundings misfortune, and poaching to guarantee the flexibility and endurance of horned species despite a quickly influencing world.

**20. Future Possibilities: Supporting Conjunction and Protection

The fate of horned species lies at the crossing point of environmental preservation, social mindfulness, and maintainable practices. Supporting conjunction among people and horned creatures includes saving territories, tending to the underlying drivers of poaching, and advancing capable the travel industry. Protection endeavors should be versatile, embracing mechanical developments, moral contemplations, and local area commitment to shield the usefulness and reason for horns for a long time into the future.

Chapter 4

Horns And Human Interaction

The cooperation among people and horns rises above simple natural capabilities, winding around a rich embroidery of social importance, utilitarian applications, and contemporary preservation challenges. Across societies and civilizations, horns have held emblematic worth, filled down to earth needs, and ignited banters about moral contemplations and preservation endeavors. This investigation dives into the complex connection among horns and human communication, following the authentic excursion from representative respect to contemporary preservation quandaries.

1. Social Imagery: Horns as Symbols of Fantasy and Religion

Horns, with their lofty structures and perplexing shapes, play played noticeable parts in the legends and religions of different societies. In antiquated Greek folklore, the god Dish was frequently portrayed with goat horns, representing ferocity and fruitfulness. Also, Celtic folklore highlighted gods like Cernunnos, embellished with tusks, addressing nature's repetitive reestablishment. Horns became intense images, typifying parts of fruitfulness, strength, and the untamed powers of the regular world.

2. Strict Iconography: Horns as Heavenly Traits

The imagery of horns reached out into strict iconography, where they were related with divine credits and profound importance. In Hinduism, the god Shiva is frequently depicted with a third eye and a sickle moon on his head, looking like a couple of horns. In Christian workmanship, horns were utilized to portray heavenly messengers and heavenly creatures, addressing strength and uprightness. The entwining of horns with strict imagery highlights their otherworldly job in forming human impression of the sacrosanct and the heavenly.

3. Stylized Antiquities: Horns in Customs and Functions

Human societies integrated horns into stylized antiquities, further underlining their representative significance. Horns were molded into instruments, like the shofar in Jewish practices, utilized in strict functions and ceremonies. The thunderous tones of these horn instruments conveyed otherworldly importance, checking sacrosanct minutes and conjuring an association between the natural and the heavenly. The use of horns in stylized settings mirrored the faith in their capacity to channel profound energies.

4. Practical Apparatuses: Horns in Day to day existence

Past their representative jobs, horns served commonsense capabilities in the regular routines of human networks. Creature horns, because of their toughness and flexibility, were designed into devices for hunting, digging, and making. Horns were utilized to make compartments, brushes, and even weapons. The innate strength and pliability of horns made them important assets for early human social orders, exhibiting an early type of feasible asset use.

5. Horned Animals: Training and Usage

The training of horned animals, like steers, goats, and sheep, denoted an essential point in mankind's set of experiences. Horns in tamed creatures filled different needs, from apparatuses in agribusiness to images of status and riches. The particular reproducing of horned animals permitted people to shape the attributes of horns for explicit capabilities, accentuating the entwining of human and creature lives during the time spent training.

6. Imagery in Workmanship and Writing: Horns as Illustrations

Horns tracked down articulation in workmanship and writing as illustrations, addressing a scope of human encounters and feelings. In middle age bestiaries, horns were frequently credited to legendary animals, representing strength, animosity, or mystical capacities. Horns became artistic gadgets, encapsulating the dualities of good and malevolence, intelligence and indiscretion. The symbolism of horns continued as a powerful image, molding social stories and imaginative portrayals.

7. Horns in Style and Embellishment: Tasteful Articulations

The tasteful allure of horns affected style and individual enhancement over the entire course of time. Horns were formed into gems, hoods, and beautifying things, reflecting individual and cultural preferences. The intricate utilization of horns in design highlighted their characteristic excellence and the human tendency to integrate regular components into individual articulations of personality and style.

8. Restorative and Ceremonial Purposes: Horns in Customary Medication

In specific societies, horns were accepted to have restorative properties, prompting their utilization in customary medication. Rhino horns, specifically, were exceptionally valued in a few Asian societies for their apparent recuperating characteristics. Notwithstanding missing logical help, the interest for rhino horns for restorative purposes has powered unlawful exchange and poaching, introducing a perplexing test for traditionalists looking to offset social convictions with untamed life security.

9. Horn Exchange and Financial Elements: Authentic Viewpoints

The verifiable exchange horns, driven by their utilitarian and emblematic worth, molded monetary elements and shipping lanes. Horns were exchanged as items, adding to the abundance and flourishing of social orders participated in business. The interest for fascinating horns, for example, those from rhinoceroses, added a layer of financial intricacy, encouraging exchange networks that traversed mainlands and filled investigation.

**10. Pioneer Abuse: Effect on Horned Species

Pioneer development frequently prompted the abuse of regular assets, including horns, with little respect for feasible practices. The interest for horned prizes and interests in the pioneer time added to the downfall of a few horned animal groups. Rhinoceroses, specifically, confronted populace declines because of territory obliteration, chasing after sport, and the exchange their horns as outlandish items.

**11. Preservation Difficulties: Rhinoceros Horns and Poaching

The protection challenges related with rhinoceros horns feature the crossing point of social convictions, financial interests, and biological conservation. The interest for rhino horns, driven by unwarranted convictions in their restorative properties, has prompted uncontrolled poaching and unlawful exchange. Preservation endeavors should address the main drivers of poaching, carry out enemy of poaching measures, and draw in neighborhood networks in the security of these notable animals.

**12. Rhino Horn Embargoes: Worldwide Reactions

Worldwide reactions to the rhino horn exchange emergency have incorporated the execution of embargoes and global participation to battle unlawful dealing. Associations and state run administrations have attempted to bring issues to light about the results of rhino poaching, implement severe enemy of poaching measures, and backer for more grounded legitimate structures to stop the unlawful exchange rhino horns.

**13. Dehorning as a Preservation Methodology: Moral Contemplations

While trying to moderate the danger of poaching, some protection drives have investigated the dubious act of dehorning rhinoceroses. Dehorning includes eliminating or managing the horns to lessen their reasonable worth and limit the impetus for poaching. Notwithstanding, dehorning raises moral contemplations, as it influences the normal ways of behaving, social elements, and natural jobs of rhinoceroses. Finding some kind of harmony between preservation needs and moral contemplations stays a complicated test.

**14. Local area Commitment: Cultivating Protection Mindfulness

Local area commitment assumes a urgent part in protection endeavors connected with horns. Cultivating mindfulness about the environmental meaning of horned species, the results of poaching, and the more extensive ramifications for biodiversity is fundamental. Drawing in nearby networks enables them to become stewards of their normal legacy and accomplices in the preservation of horned animals.

**15. The travel industry and Reasonable Works on: Adjusting Protection and Monetary Interests

The travel industry can assume a part in adjusting protection and financial interests connected with horned species. Capable the travel industry rehearses that focus on moral untamed life seeing, support neighborhood economies, and add to protection endeavors can give an elective income stream. Finding some kind of harmony between human interests and the conservation of horned species requires insightful preparation, local area inclusion, and a pledge to feasible practices.

16. Mechanical Developments: Instruments for Preservation

Mechanical developments, going from cutting edge global positioning frameworks to ramble observation, are being utilized in protection endeavors connected with horned species. These devices help in observing populaces, identifying and stopping poaching exercises, and assembling information for informed preservation methodologies. The combination of innovation into preservation rehearses exhibits the flexibility of approaches pointed toward shielding horned species and their remarkable elements.

17. Instructive Effort: Molding Points of view for Preservation

Training and effort programs are pivotal for molding viewpoints and cultivating preservation endeavors connected with horns. Bringing issues to light about the natural jobs of horns, the outcomes of poaching, and the more extensive meaning of rationing these notorious species is fundamental for gathering public help and advancing economical practices.

18. Moral Contemplations: Finding Some kind of harmony

As moderates wrestle with the difficulties of safeguarding horned species, moral contemplations come to the front. Systems, for example, dehorning, pointed toward lessening the motivation for poaching, bring up issues about the effect on normal ways of behaving and environmental jobs. Finding some kind of harmony between protection needs and moral contemplations stays a continuous test in the mission to defend these notable animals.

19. Worldwide Coordinated effort: Toward Feasible Horn Preservation

Tending to the intricacies of horn preservation requires worldwide joint effort. Global participation, research drives, and shared preservation methodologies are indispensable for guaranteeing the endurance of horned species. By joining endeavors across lines and societies, the worldwide local area can make progress toward manageable practices that safeguard these notorious animals and their one of a kind highlights.

20. Future Possibilities: Sustaining Concurrence

The eventual fate of the connection among people and horns lies in the sensitive harmony between social legacy, financial contemplations, and natural conservation. Supporting concurrence includes embracing manageable works on, encouraging mindfulness, and participating in moral ways to deal with natural life protection. As we explore the mind boggling elements of horns and human collaboration, the call to save these famous designs becomes a protection basic as well as a promise to defending the strings that interface us to the variety and miracle of the regular world.

4.1 Historical significance of rhinoceros horns

Rhinoceros horns, with their lofty and imposing appearance, have woven a rich embroidery of verifiable importance that ranges across societies, civilizations, and shipping lanes. Past their organic capabilities, rhino horns play played different parts in mankind's set of experiences, from images of force and status to fixings in conventional medication. This investigation dives into the authentic meaning of rhinoceros horns, following their way through time and unwinding the complicated strings that associate these notable designs to the records of human civilization.

1. Imagery and Power in Antiquated Human advancements

In old civic establishments, rhinoceros horns were images of force, strength, and exoticism. The uncommonness of rhinos in specific locales added to the persona encompassing their horns. In the way of life of antiquated Egypt, Greece, and Rome, rhino horns were profoundly valued as images of solidarity and virility. They tracked down their direction into the courts of rulers, where the ownership of rhino horn antiquities became markers of esteem and authority.

2. Middle age Bestiaries and Representative Symbolism

During the middle age time frame, bestiaries — outlined compositions depicting different creatures — highlighted rhinoceros horns in representative symbolism. These portrayals frequently credited legendary characteristics to the horns, giving rhinoceroses a role as fantastical animals with special powers.

The emblematic reverberation of rhino horns in archaic bestiaries added to their charm as desired objects, pursued by gatherers and sovereignty.

3. Exchange and Business in the Time of Investigation

The Period of Investigation denoted a huge section in the verifiable meaning of rhinoceros horns. European wayfarers, enthralled by the fascinating and intriguing, looked to gain rhino horns during their journeys to Africa and Asia. The prospering exchange rhino horns became entwined with the worldwide business of the time, powering request in European courts and prodding the foundation of shipping lanes to acquire these valued belongings.

4. Provincial Double-dealing and Prize Hunting

Provincial development achieved the abuse of normal assets, including rhinoceros horns. Prize hunting turned into a typical practice among provincial elites, with rhino horns pursued as images of triumph and strength. The double-dealing of rhinoceroses for their horns added to populace declines, denoting a dull period in the verifiable connection among people and these great animals.

5. Conventional Medication and Social Convictions

In specific societies, rhino horns have been profoundly imbued in conventional medication and social convictions. The horns were accepted to have mending properties, prompting their utilization in different restorative arrangements. Notwithstanding the absence of logical proof supporting these cases, the interest for rhino horns for restorative purposes persevered, impacting social practices and adding to the difficulties looked by rhino populaces.

6. East Asian Workmanship and Ancient rarities

In East Asia, rhino horns have held a remarkable spot in workmanship and curios for quite a long time. Cut rhino horn figures, known for their multifaceted subtleties and craftsmanship, became valued belongings among the tip top in China and Vietnam. These relics were esteemed for their stylish allure and were accepted to bring favorable luck, further driving the interest for rhino horns in East Asian social orders.

7. Social Imagery and Stately Purposes

Rhinoceros horns have been integrated into social imagery and stately purposes in different social orders. In a few African societies, rhino horns were formed into stately items, mirroring their social importance. The imagery related with rhino horns in these settings highlighted their job as more than simple natural extremities, becoming fundamental components of social practices and customs.

8. European Cupboards of Interests

The interest with extraordinary examples during the Renaissance period led to Cupboards of Interests, confidential assortments that housed a horde of intriguing and strange items. Rhino horns, alongside other normal miracles, tracked down their direction into these cupboards, becoming interests that enthralled the minds of researchers, gatherers, and the overall population.

9. nineteenth Century Naturalism and Logical Request

The nineteenth century saw a change in the impression of rhinoceros horns from simple interests to subjects of logical request. Naturalists and researchers started concentrating on rhinos and their horns, looking to grasp the science, life systems, and environmental jobs of these heavenly animals. This period denoted the start of a more complete comprehension of rhinoceroses past their verifiable imagery.

10. Preservation Mindfulness in the twentieth Hundred years

The twentieth century achieved expanded attention to the protection challenges confronting rhinoceros populaces. The authentic meaning of rhino horns became interwoven with pressing preservation endeavors as the acknowledgment unfolded that uncontrolled hunting, territory misfortune, and poaching were driving sure rhino species to the edge of eradication. Preservation associations and legislatures did whatever it takes to safeguard rhinos and check the unlawful exchange their horns.

11. Peaceful accords and Boycotts

Peaceful accords and boycotts assumed an essential part in tending to the exchange rhino horns. The Show on Global Exchange Imperiled Types of Wild Fauna and Vegetation (Refers to) turned into a urgent stage for managing the worldwide exchange rhino horns. Different nations established homegrown prohibitions on rhino horn exchange to control poaching and safeguard rhinoceros populaces.

12. Contemporary Difficulties and Poaching Plagues

In spite of preservation endeavors, rhinoceros populaces keep on confronting contemporary difficulties, with poaching scourges representing an extreme danger. The authentic meaning of rhino horns is currently entrapped with illegal exchange driven by request from East Asian business sectors, where rhino horns are as yet pursued for their apparent restorative properties. The disturbing ascent in poaching has ignited recharged endeavors to battle unlawful exchange and safeguard rhinoceros populaces.

**13. Dehorning as a Preservation Procedure

In light of the poaching emergency, some protection drives have investigated the disputable act of dehorning rhinoceroses. Dehorning includes eliminating or managing the horns to decrease their fairly estimated worth and limit the motivator for poaching. While dehorning has been carried out in specific districts as a preservation procedure, it raises moral contemplations and features the perplexing choices looked by progressives in their endeavors to safeguard rhinos.

**14. Local area Commitment and Economical Practices

Local area commitment has turned into a vital piece of contemporary protection techniques. Including nearby networks in protection endeavors, stressing the financial advantages of natural life the travel industry, and advancing reasonable practices are viewed as critical parts of shielding rhinoceros populaces. Adjusting the necessities of neighborhood networks with the basic to safeguard rhinos is a continuous test that requires coordinated effort and insightful methodologies.

**15. Mechanical Advancements in Protection

Mechanical developments play had a huge impact in current preservation endeavors connected with rhinos. High level global positioning frameworks, satellite innovation, and robot reconnaissance are utilized to screen rhino populaces, distinguish poaching exercises, and assemble information for informed protection procedures. The mix of innovation features the flexibility of protection approaches despite advancing difficulties.

**16. Instructive Effort and Public Mindfulness

Instructive effort projects and public mindfulness crusades have become fundamental devices in the protection tool compartment. Bringing issues to light about the authentic meaning of rhino horns, the results of poaching, and the more extensive ramifications for biodiversity is fundamental for accumulating public help. By cultivating a feeling of obligation and association with these glorious animals, instructive endeavors add to the more extensive objectives of preservation.

**17. Moral Contemplations in Protection

As traditionalists explore the perplexing scene of safeguarding rhinoceros populaces, moral contemplations come to the very front. Choices connected with dehorning, local area commitment, and economical practices require a fragile harmony between biological protection and moral standards. The moral elements of preservation highlight the requirement for a comprehensive and smart way to deal with shielding rhinos and their verifiable importance.

**18. Worldwide Cooperation for Rhinoceros Preservation

The protection of rhinoceroses requires worldwide coordinated effort. Global collaboration, research drives, and shared preservation methodologies are indispensable for guaranteeing the endurance of rhino populaces. By joining endeavors across lines and societies, the worldwide local area can pursue manageable practices that safeguard rhinos and protect the authentic meaning of their horns.

****19. Difficulties of the Anthropocene: Environmental Change and Natural surroundings Misfortune**

In the Anthropocene period, rhinoceros populaces face extra difficulties, including environmental change and territory misfortune. The effects of changing environment examples and human-prompted modifications to biological systems add layers of intricacy to protection endeavors. Tending to these interconnected difficulties is pivotal for getting the drawn out endurance of rhinoceros populaces and their authentic importance.

****20. Future Possibilities: Protecting Legacy and Biodiversity**

What's in store possibilities of rhinoceros horns and their verifiable importance lie in the aggregate endeavors of mankind. Protecting the legacy and biodiversity addressed by rhinos requires supported obligation to preservation, moral independent direction, and worldwide collaboration. As we explore the complex strings of history and protection, the conservation of rhinoceroses and their famous horns becomes an obligation as well as a demonstration of the flexibility and interconnectedness of life on The planet.

4.2 Cultural and symbolic importance

The social and emblematic meaning of rhinoceros horns rises above simple organic credits, winding around a mind boggling embroidery of implications, convictions, and practices across different human social orders. For quite a long time, these grand designs have held a significant spot in social stories, strict imagery, customary medication, and imaginative articulations. This investigation dives into the complex domain of the social and emblematic significance of rhinoceros horns, disentangling the strings that associate these notorious members to the rich texture of mankind's set of experiences and conviction frameworks.

****1. Antiquated Developments: Power and Eminence**

In the records of antiquated civic establishments, rhinoceros horns arose as images of force and esteem. The uncommonness of rhinos in specific locales pervaded their horns with a quality of exoticism, making them exceptionally desired by rulers and elites. In old Egypt, rhinoceros horns were related with the heavenly, representing strength and assurance.

The ownership of rhino horn curios became markers of power, supporting the connection between these grand animals and the progressive designs of human social orders.

****2. Folklore and Religion: Divine Credits**

The social and emblematic significance of rhinoceros horns stretched out into folklore and religion, where these designs were frequently ascribed with divine credits. In Hinduism, the goddess Lakshmi is once in a while portrayed riding a rhinoceros, connoting riches and overflow. The relationship of rhino horns with divine creatures and enormous powers added to their job in strict customs and services, laying out a significant connection between the natural and the heavenly.

3. Archaic Bestiaries: Representative Symbolism

During the archaic period, enlightened compositions known as bestiaries portrayed rhinoceros horns in representative symbolism. These representations frequently attributed legendary characteristics to rhinos, depicting them as fantastical animals with extraordinary powers. The emblematic reverberation of rhino horns in archaic bestiaries filled the creative mind of researchers and craftsmen, further implanting these designs in the social awareness.

4. Exchange and Business in the Period of Investigation

The Period of Investigation denoted a defining moment in the social meaning of rhinoceros horns, as European travelers looked for these uncommon and extraordinary fortunes during their journeys to Africa and Asia. The prospering exchange rhino horns became weaved with worldwide business, igniting interest and request in European courts. The social worth of rhino horns arrived at new levels, driving pilgrims to explore unknown regions looking for these valued belongings.

5. Pilgrim Double-dealing: Images of Success

Pilgrim extension achieved the abuse of normal assets, including rhinoceros horns. The horns became images of triumph and strength, with frontier elites participating in prize hunting and the securing of fascinating interests. The social meaning of rhino horns was interlaced with thoughts of magnificent power, denoting a time of double-dealing and exhaustion of rhino populaces.

6. Customary Medication: Mending and Folklore

In different societies, rhinoceros horns play had a vital impact in customary medication, where they were accepted to have mending properties. The horns were ground into powders or colors and used to treat a scope of sicknesses.

Notwithstanding the absence of logical proof supporting these cases, the social faith in the restorative viability of rhino horns continued, affecting customary recuperating rehearses and adding to the interest for these designs.

7. East Asian Craftsmanship and Style: Cut Tastefulness

In East Asia, rhino horns tracked down a position of high standing in craftsmanship and feel. Cut rhino horn models, known for their perplexing subtleties and craftsmanship, turned out to be profoundly valued among the world class in China and Vietnam. These ancient rarities were esteemed for their stylish allure as well as for their social imagery, accepted to bring favorable luck and flourishing. The social significance of rhino horns in East Asian social orders mirrored an amicable mix of craftsmanship, nature, and otherworldliness.

8. Social Imagery and Stylized Uses in Africa

In a few African societies, rhinoceros horns have been coordinated into social imagery and stately purposes. The horns were molded into stylized objects, mirroring their social importance. The imagery related with rhino horns in these settings highlighted their job as more than actual members, becoming necessary components of social practices and customs.

9. European Cupboards of Interests: Gatherers' Enjoyments

The interest with fascinating examples during the Renaissance period led to Cupboards of Interests, confidential assortments that housed a bunch of uncommon and strange items. Rhino horns, close by other normal miracles, tracked down their direction into these cupboards, turning into gatherers' enjoyments that spellbound the minds of researchers, blue-bloods, and the overall population. The social worth of rhino horns as interests added to their charm as images of the secretive and unprecedented.

10. nineteenth Century Naturalism: Logical Request and Representative Implications

The nineteenth century saw a change in the impression of rhinoceros horns from images of interest to subjects of logical request. Naturalists and researchers dove into the investigation of rhinos, looking to figure out the science, life systems, and biological jobs of these animals. The double idea of rhino horns — logical subjects and social images — featured the perplexing implications connected to these designs.

11. Preservation Mindfulness in the twentieth 100 years: Moving Points of view

The twentieth century achieved expanded familiarity with the preservation challenges confronting rhinoceros populaces. The social and representative significance of rhino horns became interwoven with pressing protection endeavors as the acknowledgment unfolded that uncontrolled hunting, territory misfortune, and poaching were driving sure rhino species to the edge of termination. Preservation associations and states did whatever it may take to safeguard rhinos and check the unlawful exchange their horns.

12. Peaceful accords and Boycotts: Directing Exchange

Peaceful accords and boycotts assumed an essential part in tending to the exchange rhino horns. The Show on Global Exchange Imperiled Types of Wild Fauna and Greenery (Refers to) turned into a urgent stage for controlling the worldwide exchange rhino horns. Different nations authorized homegrown restrictions on rhino horn exchange to control poaching and safeguard rhinoceros populaces.

13. Contemporary Difficulties: Poaching and Preservation Issues

In spite of preservation endeavors, rhinoceros populaces keep on confronting contemporary difficulties, with poaching pandemics representing a serious danger. The social and representative significance of rhino horns is currently caught with unlawful exchange driven by request from East Asian business sectors, where rhino horns are as yet pursued for their apparent restorative properties. The disturbing ascent in poaching has ignited reestablished endeavors to battle unlawful exchange and safeguard rhinoceros populaces.

14. Dehorning as a Preservation Technique: Moral Difficulties

In light of the poaching emergency, some preservation drives have investigated the disputable act of dehorning rhinoceroses. Dehorning includes eliminating or managing the horns to lessen their reasonable worth and limit the motivator for poaching. While dehorning has been executed in specific districts as a preservation methodology, it raises moral contemplations and features the mind boggling choices looked by moderates in their endeavors to safeguard rhinos.

**15. Local area Commitment and Supportable Works on: Adjusting Preservation and Societies

Local area commitment has turned into an indispensable piece of contemporary preservation techniques. Including nearby networks in preservation endeavors, underlining the monetary advantages of natural life the travel industry, and advancing reasonable practices are viewed as urgent parts of protecting rhinoceros populaces. Adjusting the necessities of neighborhood networks with the basic to safeguard rhinos is a continuous test that requires coordinated effort and smart methodologies.

**16. Mechanical Developments in Protection: Crossing over Past and Future

Mechanical developments play had a huge impact in present day preservation endeavors connected with rhinos. High level global positioning frameworks, satellite innovation, and robot observation are utilized to screen rhino populaces, recognize poaching exercises, and assemble information for informed protection methodologies. The mix of innovation features the versatility of preservation approaches despite developing difficulties.

**17. Instructive Effort and Public Mindfulness: Molding Points of view

Instructive effort projects and public mindfulness crusades have become crucial devices in the protection tool stash. Bringing issues to light about the social and representative significance of rhino horns, the results of poaching, and the more extensive ramifications for biodiversity is fundamental for gathering public help. By encouraging a feeling of obligation and association with these magnificent animals, instructive endeavors add to the more extensive objectives of preservation.

**18. Moral Contemplations in Preservation: Exploring Intricacy

As protectionists explore the intricate scene of safeguarding rhinoceros populaces, moral contemplations come to the front. Choices connected with dehorning, local area commitment, and maintainable practices require a sensitive harmony between environmental safeguarding and moral standards. The moral elements of protection highlight the requirement for a comprehensive and insightful way to deal with shielding rhinos and their social and representative importance.

**19. Worldwide Coordinated effort for Rhinoceros Preservation: Shared Liabilities

The preservation of rhinoceroses requires worldwide coordinated effort. Worldwide collaboration, research drives, and shared protection procedures are fundamental for guaranteeing the endurance of rhino populaces. By joining endeavors across lines and societies, the worldwide local area can make progress toward reasonable practices that safeguard rhinos and protect their social and emblematic significance.

**20. Future Possibilities: Protecting Legacy and Biodiversity

What's in store possibilities of rhinoceros horns and their social and emblematic significance lie in the aggregate endeavors of mankind. Protecting the legacy and biodiversity addressed by rhinos requires supported obligation to preservation, moral navigation, and worldwide collaboration. As we explore the unpredictable strings of history, conviction frameworks, and protection challenges, the conservation of rhinoceroses and their famous horns becomes an obligation as well as a demonstration of the versatility and interconnectedness of life on The planet.

4.3 Conservation challenges related to horn trade

The preservation challenges related with horn exchange, especially the exchange rhinoceros horns, structure an intricate and multi-layered issue. The interest for horns, driven by social convictions, customary medication rehearses, and financial interests, represents a huge danger to rhinoceros populaces worldwide. This investigation digs into the multifaceted elements of protection challenges connected with horn exchange, inspecting the convergences of social legacy, monetary inspirations, and the basic to safeguard biodiversity.

**1. Social Convictions and Customary Medication: Propagating Request

One of the essential difficulties in tending to horn exchange lies the diligence of social convictions and customary medication rehearses. Rhino horns, particularly in a few East Asian societies, are accepted to have restorative properties, notwithstanding an absence of logical proof supporting such cases. The propagation of these convictions adds to a supported interest for rhino horns, driving poaching and unlawful exchange. Protection endeavors should wrestle with the fragile undertaking of regarding social legacy while dispersing falsehood and elevating options in contrast to customary medication rehearses.

**2. Financial Interests and Poaching Motivations

The monetary impetuses related with horn exchange, especially in the bootleg market, make huge difficulties for protectionists. The high worth put on rhino horns makes them alluring focuses for poachers, who frequently exploit ruined networks with commitments of significant monetary benefits. The financial inspirations driving poaching make an endless loop, with nearby networks confronting hard decisions between protection morals and quick monetary necessities. Tending to these financial difficulties requires all encompassing methodologies that give elective jobs, advance practical the travel industry, and engage neighborhood networks to become stewards of their normal legacy.

**3. Unlawful Exchange Organizations: Refinement and Worldwide Reach

The unlawful exchange networks that work with the development of horns across borders present imposing difficulties to protection endeavors. These organizations, frequently refined and efficient, work on a worldwide scale. Endeavors to battle unlawful exchange should explore international intricacies, address debasement inside policing, and coordinate worldwide participation to destroy these organizations. Reinforcing legitimate structures and carrying out rigid measures to follow and secure those engaged with unlawful horn exchange are basic for preservation achievement.

**4. Market Interest and Shopper Conduct

The interest for horns, driven by customer conduct in specific districts, energizes the unlawful exchange and poaching emergency. Understanding and tending to the elements impacting purchaser decisions are essential parts of protection procedures. Public mindfulness crusades, designated schooling drives, and local area commitment assume key parts in moving customer conduct away from items got from horn exchange. By encouraging a feeling of obligation and moral utilization, protectionists mean to decrease interest and lessen the financial practicality of unlawful horn exchange.

**5. Emergency The board: Answering Poaching Plagues

Poaching scourges address intense preservation challenges that request quick and powerful emergency the executives. The heightening of poaching exercises, frequently energized by outside elements like monetary slumps or political shakiness, can quickly drain rhinoceros populaces. Preservation associations and states should carry out quick enemy of poaching measures, send progressed reconnaissance advances, and activate assets to safeguard weak populaces during poaching emergencies.

**6. Dehorning Situations: Moral Contemplations

The act of dehorning, which includes eliminating or managing rhino horns to lessen their fairly estimated worth and beat poaching down, is a combative preservation system. While dehorning has been carried out in specific locales as a defensive measure, it raises moral contemplations. Eliminating horns might influence the social elements, normal ways of behaving, and environmental jobs of rhinoceroses. Finding some kind of harmony between preservation needs and moral contemplations stays a test, requiring cautious evaluation of the expected effects on both rhino populaces and the biological systems they occupy.

**7. Legitimate Exchange Elements: Difficulties in Guideline

The elements of lawful horn exchange, where certain nations permit the controlled exchange of horns under managed systems, present their own arrangement of difficulties. Directing lawful exchange requires powerful frameworks to forestall spillage into the unlawful market, as horns from legitimate sources can incidentally fuel interest and subvert protection endeavors. Finding some kind of harmony between permitting feasible legitimate exchange and forestalling unlawful exercises requests powerful administration, straightforwardness, and worldwide collaboration.

**8. Worldwide Reaction: Fluctuated Responsibilities and Needs

The worldwide reaction to preservation challenges connected with horn exchange fluctuates, with nations and associations having various responsibilities and needs. While certain countries focus on tough enemy of poaching measures and promoter for complete prohibitions on horn exchange, others might seek after practical use models that license directed exchange. Crossing over these unique methodologies requires political endeavors, shared research, and a guarantee to settling on some mutual interest chasing worldwide biodiversity safeguarding.

9. Local area Commitment: Cultivating Protection Mindfulness

Drawing in neighborhood networks in protection endeavors is urgent for tending to horn exchange difficulties. Engaging people group to become dynamic members in protection, as opposed to latent onlookers, includes cultivating mindfulness about the biological meaning of rhinoceroses and the results of poaching. By advancing local area drove drives, moderates mean to construct a feeling of satisfaction in safeguarding nearby untamed life and living spaces, making a feasible starting point for biodiversity conservation.

10. The travel industry and Supportable Practices: Choices to Horn Exchange

The travel industry can act as another option and practical monetary model that mitigates the tensions of horn exchange. Mindful the travel industry rehearses, like natural life safaris and eco-accommodating hotels, add to nearby economies while focusing on preservation. Creating and advancing moral the travel industry drives diverts monetary motivating forces from horn exchange, underscoring the worth of live rhinos in their regular environments.

11. Mechanical Developments: Apparatuses for Preservation

Mechanical developments assume a critical part in tending to horn exchange difficulties. High level global positioning frameworks, satellite innovation, and robots upgrade checking and observation capacities, supporting the recognition and avoidance of poaching exercises. The incorporation of innovation into protection systems grandstands the flexibility of approaches pointed toward shielding rhinoceros populaces and disturbing unlawful exchange organizations.

12. Lawful Structures: Fortifying Securities

Reinforcing lawful structures and punishments for contribution in horn exchange is key to protection endeavors. Nations should sanction and authorize strong regulation that deflects poaching, carrying, and the offer of unlawful untamed life items.

Worldwide cooperation is fundamental for close lawful escape clauses and fit guidelines, making a bound together front against the unlawful exchange that compromises rhinoceros populaces.

13. Instruction and Mindfulness: A Drawn out Speculation

Putting resources into instruction and mindfulness programs addresses a drawn out methodology for tending to horn exchange difficulties. Instructive drives, focused on at both neighborhood networks and worldwide crowds, plan to cultivate a more profound comprehension of the natural significance of rhinoceroses and the results of horn exchange. By imparting a feeling of obligation and natural stewardship, protectionists try to make enduring social moves that help biodiversity conservation.

14. Moral Contemplations: Finding Some kind of harmony

Moral contemplations penetrate each part of protection challenges connected with horn exchange. From the choices to dehorn rhinoceroses to the execution of lawful structures and local area commitment systems, protectionists should explore a fragile harmony between social legacy, financial interests, and biological safeguarding. Finding some kind of harmony requires nonstop exchange, coordinated effort, and a pledge to arrangements that focus on the prosperity of both rhino populaces and the environments they occupy.

15. Worldwide Coordinated effort: Toward a Brought together Methodology

Addressing the protection challenges connected with horn exchange requests global coordinated effort. States, preservation associations, specialists, and networks should join to share information, assets, and best practices. A brought together methodology is fundamental for battle unlawful exchange organizations, fit lawful structures, and carry out successful preservation techniques that rise above public limits.

16. Public Promotion and Backing: Molding Approaches

Public backing and backing assume a significant part in forming strategies and impacting leaders. Preservation associations, non-administrative elements, and concerned residents can add to the talk around horn exchange by pushing for more grounded securities, moral practices, and reasonable other options. By activating general assessment, advocates become instrumental in making the political will important to execute and authorize compelling preservation measures.

17. Exploration and Advancement: Adjusting to Change

Consistent examination and advancement are essential for adjusting preservation methodologies to developing difficulties. Logical investigation into rhinoceros conduct, biological jobs, and the effect of horn exchange illuminates proof based navigation. Developments in observing advancements, natural surroundings the executives, and local area commitment methodologies add to the versatility of protection endeavors despite dynamic preservation challenges.

18. Future Possibilities: Sustaining Concurrence

What's to come possibilities of addressing protection challenges connected with horn exchange rely on supporting conjunction among people and rhinoceroses. This includes embracing moral, reasonable practices that focus on biodiversity conservation while regarding social legacy. As worldwide mindfulness develops and cooperative endeavors heighten, the expectation is to cultivate a future where rhinoceros populaces flourish, liberated from the dangers presented by illegal horn exchange.

Chapter 5

Hides And Camouflage

The many-sided universe of stows away and disguise unfurls as an embroidery woven by development, where the endurance of innumerable species depends on the craft of mixing in with their environmental elements. From the obscure examples of a leaf-followed gecko to the problematic shading of a cuttlefish, the procedures utilized by creatures to go unnoticed just by being casual are basically as different as the environments they occupy. This investigation digs into the captivating domain of stows away and cover, unwinding the systems, variations, and environmental meaning of nature's show-stoppers in camouflage.

1. Prologue to Stows away and Disguise

Stows away and disguise address nature's clever systems for endurance. The capacity to conceal really in the climate is a basic part of an organic entity's endurance tool compartment. Whether it's getting away from hunters or ambushing prey, the craft of camouflage is a dynamic and developing component across different species. Cover, in its heap structures, permits creatures to mix flawlessly with their environmental factors, giving them a critical benefit in the ceaseless weapons contest of hunter and prey.

2. Transformative Starting points: The Weapons contest of Endurance

The development of stows away and disguise is well established in the weapons contest for endurance. As hunters created more honed faculties and systems to find prey, prey species, thus, advanced modern components to stay away from identification. This co-transformative dance has brought about an astounding cluster of disguise procedures, from variety mimicry to troublesome examples, exhibiting the steadily moving harmony among tracker and chased.

3. Variety Mimicry: Mixing In with Accuracy

Variety mimicry is a typical and surprising type of disguise. Numerous species have developed to emulate the varieties and examples of their environmental factors, delivering them almost imperceptible to hunters and prey the same. The peppered moth, for instance, displays modern melanism, adjusting its shading to match the residue covered trees during the modern unrest. The chameleon, then again, is prestigious for its capacity to change tone to match its current circumstance, embodying the accuracy of variety mimicry.

4. Problematic Tinge: Separating the Diagram

Problematic tinge includes the utilization of differentiating examples and varieties to separate a creature's blueprint, making it trying for hunters or prey to observe its shape. The zebra's stripes are an exemplary illustration of problematic shading, making optical deceptions that confound hunters. Cuttlefish, bosses of mask in the sea, utilize dynamic troublesome examples to mix consistently with the moving submerged climate.

5. Foundation Coordinating: Becoming One with the Climate

Foundation matching is a cover method where a life form's hue intently matches that of its environmental factors. This methodology depends on exact variety matching to the components in the climate, making it hard for spectators to recognize the secret living being. The leaf-followed gecko, with its body looking like a dead leaf, is a momentous illustration of foundation matching in the animals of the world collectively.

6. Counter-Concealing: Playing with Light and Shadow

Counter-concealing is a type of disguise where a living being's hue is hazier on its upper side and lighter on its lower side. This transformation makes the deception of levelness, making it trying for hunters or prey to observe the three-layered type of the secret creature. The famous illustration of counter-concealing is the extraordinary white shark, whose tinge supports covert hunting from beneath.

7. Mimicry: Mixing in Through Duplicity

Mimicry includes a life form looking like one more creature or object to acquire a benefit in endurance. Batesian mimicry is the point at which an innocuous animal varieties emulates the presence of a destructive or harmful animal groups to keep away from predation. For example, the emissary butterfly emulates the shading of the harmful ruler butterfly. Müllerian mimicry happens when various unsafe species develop to look like one another, supporting an aggregate admonition signal.

8. Dynamic Disguise: Adjusting to Changing Conditions

Dynamic disguise is an entrancing variation that permits creatures to change their tinge or examples in light of evolving conditions. Cuttlefish and octopuses are experts of dynamic disguise, utilizing particular cells called chromatophores to quickly change their skin tone and surface. This transformation fills different needs, from ambushing prey to staying away from hunters progressively.

9. Secretive Way of behaving: Past Tinge

Disguise stretches out past hue to envelop secretive way of behaving, where an organic entity takes on unambiguous stances or developments to mix in with its environmental elements.

Stick bugs, for instance, mirror the presence of twigs and branches, and their unmoving conduct upgrades their cover. The katydid, looking like a leaf, shows influence mimicry, copying the development of a leaf in the breeze to stay away from location.

10. Stows away and Cover in Amphibian Conditions

The oceanic domain features a different cluster of stows away and cover methodologies adjusted to the difficulties of submerged disguise. The verdant ocean mythical serpent, with its leaf-like extremities, imitates drifting kelp, permitting it to mix flawlessly into its marine climate. The stonefish, looking like a stone on the sea floor, utilizes problematic tinge to snare clueless prey.

11. Mental Cover: Mixing In through Trickiness

Past actual transformations, a few creatures participate in mental disguise, utilizing double dealing and mimicry to show up less undermining or more interesting to expected prey or mates. The anglerfish, with its bait looking like a bioluminescent prey thing, utilizes mental disguise to draw in prey in the profound sea. Essentially, the orchid mantis emulates the presence of a bloom petal to draw in pollinators.

12. Stows away and Disguise in Human Conditions

Cover isn't restricted to the normal world; it has tracked down applications in human conditions, from military strategies to form and plan. Military disguise designs are intended to upset the diagrams of troopers in different territories, giving camouflage on the front line. Metropolitan disguise, motivated by regular types of cover, is utilized in engineering and plan to mix structures with their environmental elements.

13. Natural Importance: Adjusting Hunter Prey Elements

The natural meaning of stows away and disguise is significant, impacting hunter prey elements, populace guideline, and biodiversity. Covered prey gain an endurance advantage by staying away from predation, while hunters outfitted with powerful disguise improve their hunting achievement. The interaction among stows away and cover adds to the sensitive equilibrium of biological systems, molding the overflow and dissemination of species inside environmental networks.

14. Human Effect: Upsetting Regular Cover

Human exercises, including living space obliteration, contamination, and environmental change, present dangers to the viability of normal stows away and cover. Quick natural changes can outperform the versatile abilities of numerous species, prompting confounds between their cover systems and modified conditions. Protection endeavors assume an essential part in moderating these effects and saving the versatile benefits gave by stows away and cover.

15. Preservation Difficulties: Safeguarding Disguised Species

Protection challenges connected with stows away and disguise are unpredictably connected to the safeguarding of natural surroundings and the relief of human-incited dangers. Endeavors to safeguard covered species include territory reclamation, fighting unlawful poaching, and tending to environmental change influences. Protectionists likewise work to bring issues to light about the biological significance of stows away and cover, cultivating a more profound comprehension of the interconnectedness of species in their regular habitats.

16. Mechanical Bits of knowledge: Biomimicry and Disguise Developments

Mechanical progressions propelled by normal stows away and disguise have prompted developments in different fields. Biomimicry, drawing motivation from nature's plans, has impacted the advancement of versatile disguise materials and innovations. These developments track down applications in military advances, wearable disguise, and compositional plans that consolidate standards of regular camouflage.

17. Moral Contemplations: Adjusting Human Interests and Natural life Insurance

As people proceed to investigate and use regular assets, moral contemplations encompassing stows away and cover come to the very front. Adjusting human interests, like land improvement and asset extraction, with the need to safeguard covered species requires smart and maintainable practices. Preservation morals assume a vital part in directing choices that influence the sensitive balance between human exercises and the endurance of disguised organic entities.

18. Instructive Drives: Cultivating Appreciation for Cover

Instructive drives are fundamental for encouraging appreciation for stows away and cover, both in regular biological systems and human-planned conditions. By expanding public mindfulness about the complexities of disguise methodologies and the significance of protecting biodiversity, schooling turns into an integral asset for rousing preservation activity and advancing reasonable conjunction with covered species.

19. Worldwide Cooperation: A Bound together Way to deal with Protection

The preservation of covered species requires worldwide cooperation. Worldwide participation, research drives, and shared protection methodologies are essential for guaranteeing the endurance of species depending on stows away and disguise. By joining endeavors across lines and societies, the worldwide local area can pursue reasonable practices that safeguard disguised creatures and save the complicated woven artwork of nature's covering systems.

20. Future Points of view: Coinciding with Covered Miracles

The future points of view of stows away and cover lie in our aggregate obligation to coinciding with the miracles of nature. As we advance in mechanical development and extend how we might interpret environmental interdependencies, the safeguarding of stows away and cover becomes a preservation basic as well as a demonstration of our obligation as stewards of the different and captivating embroidery of life on The planet.

5.1 Skin structure and composition

The skin, our body's biggest organ, fills in as a surprising and flexible safeguard that safeguards against outer dangers while assuming an essential part in different physiological capabilities. Its construction and structure mirror an intricate embroidery of interconnected layers, cells, and parts that add to its versatility and flexibility. This investigation digs into the unpredictable universe of skin design and sythesis, disclosing the mysteries of this complex organ that isn't just our actual hindrance yet additionally a powerful connection point between the inner and outer conditions.

1. **Prologue to the Skin: Our Dynamic Safeguard**
   The skin, or integumentary framework, is a perplexing organ that fills in as a defensive safeguard for the body. Including the epidermis, dermis, and hypodermis, the skin goes about as a boundary against actual injury, microbes, and hurtful natural components. Past its defensive capability, the skin is engaged with tactile insight, temperature guideline, and the combination of vitamin D.

2. **Epidermis: The Furthest Layer**
   The epidermis frames the furthest layer of the skin and is fundamentally made out of defined squamous epithelial tissue. This layer is in direct contact with the outside climate, making it a vital part of the body's guard framework. The epidermis is additionally separated into a few sublayers, including the layer corneum, layer granulosum, layer spinosum, and layer basale.
   Layer Corneum: The furthest layer, comprising of smoothed, keratinized cells, goes about as a defensive boundary against drying out and ecological stressors.
   Layer Granulosum: Underneath the layer corneum, this layer contains granular cells that add to the development of lipids, fundamental for skin hydration.
   Layer Spinosum: Described by spiky projections on cell surfaces, this layer offers underlying help and aids the combination of keratin, a sinewy protein.
   Layer Basale: The deepest layer, where cells go through dynamic division, guaranteeing a constant recharging of the epidermal layers.

3. **Keratinocytes: Building Blocks of the Epidermis**
   Keratinocytes, the transcendent cells in the epidermis, are liable for the development of keratin, a sinewy protein that grants strength and flexibility to the skin. As keratinocytes relocate from the layer basale to the layer corneum, they go through a course of keratinization, changing into solid, waterproof cells that structure the defensive boundary of the skin.

4. **Melanocytes: Watchmen of Pigmentation**
   Melanocytes, situated in the layer basale, assume a crucial part in skin shading. These specific cells produce melanin, the shade liable for different shades of skin, hair, and eye tone. Melanin gives insurance against the unsafe impacts of bright (UV) radiation by retaining and dispersing UV beams.

5. **Langerhans Cells and Merkel Cells: Sentinels and Contact Receptors**
   Langerhans cells, dissipated all through the epidermis, are invulnerable cells that capability as sentinels, identifying and answering potential dangers like microbes. Merkel cells, found in the layer basale, act as contact receptors, adding to the tactile elements of the skin.

6. **Dermis: The Steady Center Layer**
Underneath the epidermis lies the dermis, a connective tissue layer wealthy in veins, nerves, and different specific designs. Made out of collagen and flexible strands, the dermis offers underlying help, versatility, and sustenance to the skin. It houses hair follicles, sweat organs, sebaceous organs, veins, and sensitive spots.
Collagen and Versatile Filaments: Collagen strands offer rigidity, keeping the skin from tearing, while flexible filaments give adaptability and strength.
Veins: The dermal veins supply supplements and oxygen to the skin cells, working with cell works and fix processes.
Hair Follicles: Implanted in the dermis, hair follicles are structures that produce hair and are related with sebaceous (oil) organs.
Sweat Organs: Sweat organs, including eccrine and apocrine organs, are answerable for controlling internal heat level and discharging side-effects.
Sebaceous Organs: Sebaceous organs produce sebum, a slick substance that greases up the skin and hair, forestalling parchedness and offering a level of antibacterial insurance.
Sensitive spots: The dermis is lavishly innervated, facilitating tangible receptors that identify different boosts, including contact, strain, agony, and temperature.

7. **Hypodermis: The Subcutaneous Layer**
The hypodermis, otherwise called the subcutaneous layer, lies underneath the dermis and fills in as a connective tissue layer associating the skin to hidden tissues, muscles, and bones. It contains fat (fat) tissue, veins, and nerves. The hypodermis capabilities as a cover, giving warm guideline and filling in as an energy supply.

8. **Fat Tissue: Energy Stockpiling and Warm Guideline**
Fat tissue in the hypodermis fills in as a repository for energy capacity as fatty substances. Past its part in digestion, fat tissue adds to protection, directing internal heat level by going about as a warm cradle.

9. **Blood Supply and Supplement Trade**
The skin's broad organization of veins, including conduits, veins, and vessels, assumes a fundamental part in supplement trade, squander expulsion, and temperature guideline. Veins convey oxygen and supplements to skin cells, support safe reactions, and help with keeping up with homeostasis.

10. **Sensory system Joining: Tangible Insight and Reaction**
The skin is complicatedly associated with the sensory system, with tangible receptors identifying different upgrades and transferring signs to the cerebrum. Mechanoreceptors answer mechanical boosts like touch and strain, thermoreceptors identify temperature changes, and nociceptors sense torment. This mix considers fast reactions to ecological signals, guaranteeing the body's versatile endurance.

11. **Skin Extremities: Hair, Nails, and Organs**
Skin extremities, including hair, nails, and different organs, are gotten from the epidermis and have explicit capabilities connected with insurance, sensation, and thermoregulation.
Hair: Hair follicles produce hair, which fills in as protection, security against UV radiation, and a tactile capability through the recognition of air developments.
Nails: Nails, made out of keratinized cells, safeguard the fingertips and upgrade fine touch sensations. They additionally act as marks of by and large wellbeing.
Sweat Organs: Eccrine perspiration organs manage internal heat level by creating a watery emission, while apocrine perspiration organs, found in regions with thick hair follicles, discharge a thicker emission impacted by pressure and feelings.
Sebaceous Organs: Sebaceous organs produce sebum, an oil that greases up the skin and hair, forestalling lack of hydration and offering a level of antibacterial insurance.

12. **Skin Improvement and Mending: A Regenerative Excursion**
The skin goes through steady recharging and fix processes over the course of life. The regenerative limit of the epidermis empowers the recuperating of wounds, cuts, and scraped areas. Cell turnover, driven by the expansion of basal cells in the layer basale, guarantees a constant renewal of the epidermal layers.

13. **Factors Influencing Skin Wellbeing: Outer and Interior Impacts**
A few elements, both inside and outer, impact skin wellbeing. Extraneous variables incorporate openness to UV radiation, ecological poisons, and cruel synthetics, while characteristic elements include hereditary inclinations, hormonal changes, and in general wellbeing. Keeping up with skin wellbeing includes defensive measures, like sun security, hydration, and a decent eating routine.

14. **Skin Sicknesses and Issues: Difficulties to Homeostasis**
Different skin illnesses and problems can disturb the multifaceted harmony between the skin's design and capability. Conditions like dermatitis, psoriasis, skin inflammation, and skin tumors feature the weakness of the skin to irritation, contamination, and harmful changes. Understanding the fundamental instruments of these problems is fundamental for powerful finding and treatment.

15. **Maturing and Skin: Exploring the Inescapable Changes**
Maturing is joined by changes in skin design and capability. Collagen and elastin filaments decrease, prompting wrinkles and drooping. Diminished oil creation and more slow cell turnover add to dryness and a decrease in skin flexibility. Understanding the physiological changes related with maturing illuminates skincare rehearses that advance skin wellbeing and versatility.

16. **Skin health management: Supporting the Defensive Boundary**
Viable healthy skin includes a comprehensive methodology that thinks about both interior and outside factors. Practices like normal purging, saturating, sun

security, and a decent eating routine add to keeping up with the skin's wellbeing and imperativeness. Fitting skincare schedules to individual skin types and needs upgrades the defensive elements of the skin.

17. **Propels in Dermatology: Advancements in Skin Wellbeing**

    Progresses in dermatology keep on unwinding new bits of knowledge into skin wellbeing and proposition imaginative ways to deal with address different skin conditions. From the improvement of designated treatments for skin tumors to progressions in surface level dermatology, examination and innovation assume a critical part in upgrading how we might interpret the skin's intricacies.

18. **Moral Contemplations in Skincare: Adjusting Feel and Wellbeing**

    Chasing after skincare and restorative mediations, moral contemplations come to the very front. Finding some kind of harmony between tasteful objectives and keeping up with skin wellbeing includes informed navigation, straightforwardness in item details, and adherence to moral practices in the skincare business.

19. **Future Boondocks in Dermatology: Arising Patterns and Potential outcomes**

The eventual fate of dermatology holds invigorating conceivable outcomes, from customized skincare in view of hereditary profiles to imaginative medicines for skin illnesses. Examination into regenerative medication, bioengineering, and the microbiome's effect on skin wellbeing opens new outskirts in getting it and upgrading the skin's versatility.

5.2 Adaptive coloration for different environments

In the huge embroidery of the normal world, organic entities have developed a bunch of versatile tinge methodologies to explore and flourish in different conditions. From the enigmatic shades of chameleons mixing flawlessly with vegetation to the energetic advance notice signs of harmful frogs, versatile hue is a dynamic and fundamental part of endurance. This investigation digs into the captivating domain of versatile shading, disentangling the mind boggling manners by which living beings utilize variety to cover, convey, and eventually secure their position in the perplexing dance of biological systems.

1. **Prologue to Versatile Hue: A Range of Endurance Strategies**

    Versatile hue alludes to the capacity of living beings to adjust their variety or examples to suit the particular requests of their current circumstance. This developmental peculiarity is a demonstration of the many-sided transaction among life forms and their environmental factors, enveloping a scope of systems that improve endurance, proliferation, and by and large wellness. Whether it's hiding themselves from hunters or motioning toward likely mates, living beings have tackled the force of variety to explore the difficulties of their separate territories.

2. **Foundation Coordinating: Mixing into the Material**

   One of the essential versatile shading methodologies is foundation coordinating, where life forms impersonate the varieties and examples of their environmental elements to become subtle. This type of disguise is predominant across different conditions, from the stripes of a tiger mixing into tall grasses to the complicated examples on a moth's wings reflecting the surface of tree husk. The progress of foundation matching lies in the creature's capacity to take advantage of obvious signs and really vanish into its environment.

3. **Counter-Concealing: Playing with Light and Shadow**

   Counter-concealing is one more versatile shading procedure utilized by various species. In this method, life forms display more obscure shading on their upper side and lighter hue on their lower side. This makes an optical deception that decreases shadows, making it challenging for hunters or prey to perceive the three-layered type of the living being. Famous models incorporate the extraordinary white shark, whose counter-concealed shading helps with covert hunting from underneath.

4. **Problematic Shading: Separating the Diagram**

   Troublesome shading includes the utilization of differentiating examples and varieties to separate an organic entity's blueprint, making it trying for hunters or prey to see its actual shape. The zebra's unmistakable stripes are an exemplary illustration of troublesome hue, making visual disarray for hunters like lions. Additionally, bugs like the peppered moth utilize troublesome hue to mix with the surfaces of their environmental factors, keeping away from recognition by hunters.

5. **Mimicry: Misleading Impersonation for Endurance**

   Mimicry is a modern versatile tinge methodology where living beings mirror the presence of another species, item, or component in their current circumstance. This can fill different needs, including keeping away from predation, getting prey, or accessing assets.

   Batesian mimicry includes an innocuous animal groups impersonating the presence of a destructive or harmful animal varieties, acquiring security from likely hunters. The emissary butterfly imitating the poisonous ruler butterfly is an exemplary model.

6. **Variety Change: Dynamic Transformations for Various Conditions**

   A creatures have the exceptional capacity to change their variety in light of natural signals or improvements. Chameleons, for example, are eminent for their capacity to adjust their skin tone to coordinate their environmental elements or speak with different chameleons. Cuttlefish, cephalopods found in marine conditions, utilize specific cells called chromatophores to quickly change their skin tone and example, empowering them to explore a range of submerged conditions.

7. **Aposematism: Cautioning Signs in Clear Tones**
   Rather than camouflage procedures, aposematism includes living beings showing dynamic and prominent tinge as an advance notice signal. This tinge fills in as an impediment to likely hunters, demonstrating that the creature has unsafe or harmful guards. Poison dart frogs in tropical rainforests, with their striking and different varieties, epitomize aposematism, flagging their harmfulness and deterring hunters from endeavoring to consume them.

8. **Occasional Variations: Nature's Closet Changes**
   Occasional changes present one of a kind difficulties for organic entities, inciting numerous to go through versatile hue to match their current circumstance's moving tints. Icy creatures, for example, the Cold fox and ptarmigan, progress from brown or dark in the late spring to white in the colder time of year, giving powerful cover against the blanketed scene. This occasional transformation supports disguise as well as mirrors the life forms' capacity to synchronize with the evolving seasons.

9. **Oceanic Disguise: Mixing Underneath the Waves**
   In oceanic conditions, versatile hue takes on extraordinary structures to work with covering, hunting, and correspondence. Marine creatures frequently show countershading to mix with the changing light circumstances in the water segment. Also, cephalopods like octopuses and cuttlefish are bosses of oceanic disguise, utilizing chromatophores to emulate the varieties and examples of the ocean bottom or encompassing coral reefs.

10. **Bright Variations: Past Human Insight**
    While people see a restricted scope of varieties, numerous living beings have transformations that reach out into the bright (UV) range. A few blossoms, for instance, show UV designs undetectable to the natural eye however act as guides for pollinators. Honey bees, which can find in the UV range, are attracted to these examples, featuring the mind boggling manners by which versatile hue rises above the noticeable range.

11. **Biofluorescence and Bioluminescence: Enlightening Transformations**
    In the profundities of the sea, where daylight battles to enter, creatures have advanced biofluorescence and bioluminescence as versatile hue techniques. Biofluorescent creatures ingest light at one frequency and yet again transmit it at a more extended frequency, making a brilliant presentation. Bioluminescence includes the creation of light through synthetic responses, permitting organic entities like jellyfish and certain fish to emanate their own brightening, serving capabilities from drawing in mates to preventing hunters.

12. **Human Effect on Versatile Shading: Interruption and Preservation Difficulties**
    Human exercises, including living space obliteration, contamination, and environmental change, present critical dangers to life forms depending on versatile

tinge. Disturbance of normal living spaces, presentation of obtrusive species, and changes in environment examples can challenge the adequacy of versatile hue, prompting bungles among organic entities and their surroundings. Protection endeavors assume a urgent part in moderating these effects and saving the complicated variations that work with endurance.

13. **Mechanical Applications: Gaining from Nature's Range**

The investigation of versatile shading in nature has propelled mechanical developments with applications in different fields. Impersonating nature's methodologies, scientists have created versatile cover materials for military use, compositional plans that integrate energy-productive cooling roused by creature transformations, and sensors in view of the standards of creature vision. These biomimetic approaches grandstand the potential for manageable arrangements roused by the regular world.

14. **Moral Contemplations: Adjusting Perception and Protection**

As researchers and aficionados concentrate on versatile shading, moral contemplations emerge concerning the effect of human perception on normal environments. Practices like ecotourism and natural life photography, while giving open doors to schooling and appreciation, ought to be led mindfully to limit aggravation and stress to the organic entities being noticed. Adjusting the craving for information with the basic of preservation is fundamental for the drawn out prosperity of environments.

15. **Future Boondocks in Versatile Shading Exploration: Unwinding Nature's Secrets**

The fate of versatile shading research holds energizing possibilities, powered by headways in innovation, hereditary qualities, and environmental comprehension. Incorporating sub-atomic investigations, field studies, and man-made reasoning, analysts intend to unwind the hereditary premise of versatile tinge, investigate the environmental results of variety changes, and apply this information to protection and maintainability endeavors.

5.3 Role of hides in rhinoceros survival

In the many-sided embroidery of the collective of animals, rhinoceroses stand as considerable and notorious figures, formed by development to explore different scenes and environments. Vital to their step by step process for surviving is the exceptional transformation of their stows away, filling in as a multi-layered shroud that gives security, correspondence, and thermoregulation. This investigation dives into the essential job of conceals in rhinoceros endurance, unwinding the complexities of this basic part of their developmental excursion.

1. **The Developmental Meaning of Rhino Stows away**

The stows away of rhinoceroses, contained thick and tough skin, are a result of millions of long stretches of transformative refinement. The unmistakable over-lays, wrinkles, and examples on their stows away are a demonstration of their hereditary history as well as an essential variation that improves their possibilities of endurance in testing conditions. Development has molded rhino stows away to be an imposing protection against different dangers, denoting the crossing point of hereditary qualities, environment, and methods for surviving.

2. **Actual Assurance: The Protection of Toughness**

   One of the essential elements of rhino stows away is to give actual insurance against outside dangers. The thick, hard skin goes about as a characteristic re-inforcement, safeguarding rhinoceroses from scraped spots, wounds, and the nibbles of bugs and parasites. This variation is particularly essential in their living spaces, which can incorporate thick vegetation, rough territories, and regions with expected dangers. The conceal fills in as a hearty hindrance that empowers rhinos to explore and get through testing scenes.

3. **Disguise and Obscure Hue: Merging with the Climate**

   Rhinoceros stows away contribute fundamentally to their capacity to mix into their environmental elements through a type of cover known as mysterious shading. The variety and surface of their stows away permit them to become un-noticeable in their regular territories, giving a layer of security against hunters. In verdant savannas, the dim earthy colored tints of their stows away make a consistent mix with the encompassing vegetation, offering a strategic benefit in staying away from recognition.

4. **Thermoregulation: Cooling Systems in the Intensity**

   The conditions possessed by rhinoceroses can be portrayed by outrageous tem-peratures, going from searing intensity to crisp evenings. The conceals assume a significant part in the thermoregulation of rhinos, assisting them with dealing with their internal heat level successfully. The exceptional overlap and wrinkles in their skin make surface region varieties that guide in dispersing heat through evaporative cooling. Furthermore, the thickness of their stows away gives protec-tion against the chilly, guaranteeing that rhinos can keep up with ideal internal heat level in assorted climatic circumstances.

5. **Correspondence and Social Elements: Stows away as Flagging Stages**

   Rhinoceroses are not single animals; numerous species show social ways of be-having and structure complex collaborations inside their gatherings. The stows away of rhinos assume a part in correspondence and motioning inside these social designs. Predominant guys, for instance, may utilize their stows away to pass data about their status and affirm strength on through presentations and conflicts. The surface, shading, and even fragrance of their conceals become fundamental components in the mind boggling language of rhinoceros corre-spondence.

6. **Aroma Checking: An engraving Area and Conceptive Flagging**

   Past the noticeable elements, the stows away of rhinoceroses are instrumental in fragrance denoting, a way of behaving essential for portraying an area and flagging conceptive preparation. Specific organs on their conceals discharge emissions that convey exceptional synthetic marks, permitting rhinos to stamp their presence in the climate. This olfactory correspondence is especially huge during the rearing season, as guys and females use aroma markings to pass on data about their conceptive status and accessibility.

7. **Social Acknowledgment: Distinguishing People through Stows away**

   The peculiarity of rhino stows away stretches out to individual acknowledgment inside gatherings. Similarly as human fingerprints are interesting, the examples and highlights on rhinoceros stows away are well defined for every person.

   This peculiarity supports social attachment, permitting rhinos to perceive and connect with recognizable people inside their gatherings. The capacity to recognize each other through visual and olfactory signs on their conceals cultivates agreeable ways of behaving and builds up friendly bonds.

8. **Weaknesses and Dangers: The Stow away as an Objective**

   While the stows away of rhinoceroses act as a safeguard against numerous natural difficulties, they likewise become an objective for one of the main dangers to their endurance: poaching. The interest for rhino horns, driven by misinformed convictions in their restorative properties and social importance, has prompted an overwhelming unlawful exchange. Poachers explicitly focus on the rhino's stow away to access and eliminate the horns, bringing about serious ramifications for rhino populaces around the world.

9. **Human Preservation Endeavors: Safeguarding Rhinos from Abuse**

   Traditionalists and untamed life associations play perceived the basic part of rhino conceals in the endurance of these sublime animals. Endeavors to shield rhinos from poaching incorporate enemy of poaching watches, untamed life safe-havens, and the execution of innovative arrangements, for example, rhino GPS beacons. Protection drives likewise include local area commitment, training, and global joint effort to address the main drivers of rhino double-dealing.

10. **Protection Difficulties and Arrangements: Adjusting Human and Rhino Needs**

    Rationing rhinos requires a sensitive harmony between the necessities of nearby networks, financial interests, and the basic to safeguard these jeopardized species. Human-natural life struggle acts difficulties like rhinos might wander into farming regions, prompting conflicts with networks. Supportable improvement rehearses, local area based protection drives, and moral the travel industry can add to cultivating concordance between human populaces and rhinoceros natural surroundings.

11. **The Fate of Rhino Preservation: Sustaining a Concurrent Future**

The fate of rhino protection depends on a diverse methodology that envelops territory conservation, hostile to poaching endeavors, local area contribution, and worldwide support. As we endeavor to safeguard the conceals that have been vital to rhino endurance for a long period of time, we likewise perceive the interconnectedness of biological systems and the requirement for moral and maintainable practices that guarantee the persevering through conjunction of rhinoceroses and the normal world.

Chapter 6

Communication Through Body Language

In the huge domain of human communication, words are only one piece of the complex language we use to convey contemplations, feelings, and aims. Similarly, while possibly not all the more remarkable, is the quiet orchestra of non-verbal communication — a complex and nuanced type of non-verbal correspondence that says a lot without expressing a solitary word. This investigation dives into the complex universe of non-verbal communication, disentangling its importance, comprehensiveness, social subtleties, and the significant effect it has on human connections and understanding.

1. **The All inclusiveness of Non-verbal communication: A Culturally diverse Vocabulary**

   Non-verbal communication is an all inclusive language that rises above etymological and social limits. Across various social orders and networks, certain non-verbal prompts convey comparative implications, established in shared human encounters and feelings. Looks, motions, stance, and even eye to eye connection structure a diverse vocabulary that empowers individuals to see each other on a more profound, more intuitive level. The comprehensiveness of non-verbal communication features its basic roots in human development and the central ways it helps with correspondence.

2. **Looks: The Material of Feelings**

   The face is a material that lays out the scene of our feelings. Looks, whether an unobtrusive jerk of the lips or a wrinkling of the forehead, impart a range of sentiments — from happiness and shock to outrage and trouble. Generally perceived looks, for example, a grin showing joy or wrinkled temples flagging concern, establish the groundwork for sympathetic associations among individuals, cultivating close to home reverberation and understanding.

3. **Motions: Quiet Discussions with Our Hands**

   Motions are a necessary piece of non-verbal communication, permitting people to articulate their thoughts, explain explanations, or underline focuses. While explicit signals might have social varieties, many are all around comprehended. A thumbs-up motion implies endorsement or understanding in different societies, while a raised forefinger might flag a place of accentuation or a solicitation for consideration. The force of signals lies in their capacity to add profundity and lucidity to verbal correspondence, filling in as a quiet ally to expressed words.

4. **Stance and Body Developments: The Syntax of Presence**

   The manner in which we convey ourselves, our stance, and our body developments add to the punctuation of non-verbal communication, molding the general message we pass on. An individual who stands tall with an open stance might ooze certainty and transparency, while somebody slouched over may convey weakness or distress. Body developments, for example, inclining forward to communicate interest or crossing arms to flag protectiveness, make a powerful layer of correspondence that expands verbal articulation.

5. **Eye to eye connection: The Doorway to Association**

   Eye to eye connection is a strong and personal type of non-verbal correspondence. It fills in as a passage to association, laying out compatibility, trust, and understanding between people. Supported eye to eye connection during a discussion signals mindfulness and commitment, cultivating a feeling of association and common regard. On the other hand, staying away from eye to eye connection might convey uneasiness, modesty, or an absence of certainty. The eyes, frequently alluded to as the windows to the spirit, uncover volumes about our feelings and aims.

6. **Proxemics: Exploring Individual Space**

   Proxemics, the investigation of individual space, adds one more layer to the many-sided dance of non-verbal communication. Various societies have shifting standards and assumptions about private space, impacting how people associate. Understanding and regarding proxemics add to successful correspondence, as attacking individual space can prompt inconvenience or strain, while keeping a suitable separation cultivates a feeling of solace and common regard.

7. **Microexpressions: Flicker and-You-Miss-It Minutes**

   Microexpressions are transitory looks that last just a negligible portion of a second, frequently uncovering certified feelings that people might endeavor to intentionally cover. These unpretentious, compulsory developments can give experiences into an individual's actual sentiments, in any event, when they are attempting to veil their feelings. The capacity to perceive and decipher microexpressions improves the ability to appreciate people on a profound level, empowering people to explore social connections with elevated responsiveness.

8. **Social Subtleties: Deciphering the Quiet Tongues**

   While specific parts of non-verbal communication are generally perceived, social subtleties essentially impact translation. Motions, stances, and looks might convey changed implications or importance across societies. What is viewed as a cordial signal in one culture may be seen distinctively in another. Attention to these social subtleties is pivotal for successful multifaceted correspondence, forestalling mistaken assumptions and cultivating social capability.

9. **Distinctions in sexual orientation: Revealing the Social Content**

   Orientation assumes a part in forming non-verbal communication, reflecting cultural assumptions and standards. From the manner in which people sit to the utilization of signals and articulations, there are much of the time unpretentious orientation explicit prompts implanted in non-verbal communication. Consciousness of these subtleties is fundamental for destroying generalizations and advancing fair correspondence, permitting people to put themselves out there really without adjusting to unbending cultural contents.

10. **Non-verbal communication in Proficient Settings: Power Elements and Impressions**

    In proficient settings, non-verbal communication can altogether affect view of skill, authority, and reliability. Sure stance, confident handshakes, and kept in touch can add to positive impressions, while slumping, squirming, or keeping away from eye to eye connection might convey vulnerability or absence of certainty. Understanding the subtleties of expert non-verbal communication is instrumental in exploring the intricacies of working environment elements and correspondence.

11. **Tricky Non-verbal communication: Figuring out the real story**

    While non-verbal communication is much of the time a certified impression of contemplations and feelings, people may likewise utilize tricky non-verbal communication to veil their actual sentiments or goals. Conflicting motions, constrained grins, or keeping away from eye to eye connection can be marks of duplicity. Perceiving these signals, frequently alluded to as "tells," is fundamental for knowing credibility in relational communications and exchanges.

12. **Non-verbal communication in Connections: The Dance of Closeness**

    In close connections, non-verbal communication turns into a nuanced dance that conveys love, fondness, and association. From the delicate dash of a hand to the unobtrusive slant of the head, couples foster their own quiet language that develops close to home bonds.

    Alternately, negative non-verbal communication, like crossed arms or dismissed act, can flag strain or disengagement. Supporting positive non-verbal communication is essential to building and supporting sound connections.

13. **The Effect of Innovation: Exploring Virtual Non-verbal communication**

    In an undeniably computerized world, where correspondence frequently happens through screens, the elements of non-verbal communication have developed. Virtual non-verbal communication remembers components, for example, looks for video calls, the utilization of emoticons in instant messages, and, surprisingly, the decision of profile pictures via web-based entertainment. While these signs may not recreate the lavishness of in-person communications, they actually assume a vital part in conveying feelings and goals in the computerized domain.

14. **Improving Relational abilities: The Craft of Careful Articulation**
Creating successful relational abilities includes developing care in both verbal and non-verbal articulation. Focusing on one's own non-verbal communication, being sensitive to the non-verbal signals of others, and rehearsing undivided attention add to improved relational correspondence. The specialty of careful articulation includes adjusting verbal and non-verbal messages to make bona fide, conscious, and compassionate collaborations.

15. **Non-verbal communication Openly Speaking: The Coordination of Presence**

Public talking requires a dominance of non-verbal communication to draw in, convince, and spellbind a crowd of people. From sure walks in front of an audience to deliberate signals that accentuate central issues, compelling speakers tackle the force of non-verbal communication to convey authority and associate with their audience members. The organization of presence through non-verbal communication is an expertise that can be sharpened to leave an enduring effect on crowds.

6.1 Understanding rhinoceros behavior
Rhinoceroses, the magnificent goliaths of the savannas and backwoods, display an intriguing cluster of ways of behaving that mirror their complicated social designs, versatile methodologies, and reactions to their surroundings. Noticing and grasping rhinoceros conduct is vital for preservation endeavors, as it gives bits of knowledge into their requirements, difficulties, and generally speaking prosperity. This investigation digs into the multi-layered universe of rhinoceros conduct, revealing insight into their correspondence, social elements, proliferation, and the different variables impacting their lives in nature.

1. **Social Designs: The Elements of Rhino People group**
Rhinoceroses are social creatures, and their social designs change among species. White rhinoceroses (Ceratotherium simum), for example, are known for shaping greater gatherings, frequently alluded to as accidents, which might comprise of numerous people. Dark rhinoceroses (Diceros bicornis), then again, are by and large more singular, with people basically partner for the end goal of mating. Inside an accident of white rhinos, a prevailing male, frequently alluded to as a bull, may lead the gathering. Female white rhinos and their calves structure

a center piece of the accident, making an organized social ordered progression. Notwithstanding being more lone, dark rhinos additionally show regional ways of behaving, with covering home ranges that might prompt periodic experiences between people.

Understanding the elements inside rhino social designs is imperative for progressives, as interruptions can affect rearing, regional ways of behaving, and by and large populace wellbeing.

2. **Correspondence through Vocalizations: The Inconspicuous Language of Rhinos**

While rhinoceroses are not referred to for their vocalizations as much as some other African megafauna, they in all actuality do impart through different sounds. Rhinos produce snorts, grunts, and blares, which act as an inconspicuous language among people. These vocalizations can pass on data about their mind-set, aims, or expected dangers.

Calves might speak with their moms through particular calls, and prevailing bulls might utilize vocalizations to affirm their strength or express their presence to different rhinos nearby. Understanding these unpretentious signs is fundamental for specialists and preservationists looking to translate the subtleties of rhino correspondence and conduct.

3. **Regional Ways of behaving: Shielding Home Reaches and Assets**

Rhinoceroses, especially dark rhinos, show regional ways of behaving to lay out and protect home reaches. These regions contain fundamental assets like food, water, and appropriate rearing regions. Male rhinos are especially regional, denoting their limits with excrement heaps and pee as an approach to conveying possession and discouraging likely gatecrashers.

Regional questions between rhinos, particularly guys, can prompt showdowns, where people might participate in showcases of strength, vocalizations, and, surprisingly, actual conflicts. These regional ways of behaving are critical for keeping up with environmental equilibrium and guaranteeing that rhinos approach the assets required for their endurance.

4. **Taking care of Propensities: The Herbivorous Way of life of Rhinos**

Rhinoceroses are herbivores with particular taking care of propensities that shift among species. White rhinos are nibblers, principally consuming grasses, while dark rhinos are programs, benefiting from various woody plants and bushes. The construction of their mouths and lips mirrors these dietary inclinations, with white rhinos having more extensive, square-molded mouths adjusted for touching, and dark rhinos having more pointed, snared lips appropriate for getting a handle on foliage.

Understanding the dietary propensities for rhinos is significant for preservation endeavors, as it helps with living space the executives and guarantees that safeguarded regions can uphold the wholesome necessities of rhino populaces.

5. **Conceptive Ways of behaving: Romance, Mating, and Parental Consideration**

   Regenerative ways of behaving assume a critical part in the existences of rhinoceroses. Mating customs frequently include romance showcases, vocalizations, and actual connections among guys and females. Female rhinos might show responsive ways of behaving, demonstrating their preparation to mate. During mating, the pair participates in fornication, which might happen a few times before the female considers.

   Growth periods fluctuate among rhino species, with white rhinos having a more extended incubation period contrasted with dark rhinos. Female rhinos are for the most part mindful moms, giving consideration and security to their calves. Understanding these regenerative ways of behaving is pivotal for overseeing rearing projects in imprisonment and guaranteeing the conceptive outcome of wild populaces.

6. **Transformations to Natural Variables: Adapting to Difficulties**

   Rhinoceroses have developed different social transformations to adapt to natural difficulties. For example, their floundering conduct, where they roll in mud, fills various needs. Floundering assists rhinos with controlling internal heat level by cooling their skin, shields them from sun related burn and bug nibbles, and makes a layer of mud that goes about as a characteristic sunscreen.

   Moreover, rhinos might utilize explicit natural surroundings and transient examples to follow occasional changes in vegetation and water accessibility. Noticing these versatile ways of behaving gives important experiences into how rhinos explore their biological systems and adapt to natural changes.

7. **Human-Natural life Struggle: Figuring out Forceful Ways of behaving**

   In locales where human populaces infringe upon rhino natural surroundings, there is an improved probability of human-untamed life struggle. Rhinoceroses might show forceful ways of behaving because of seen dangers or unsettling influences. Charges, where a rhino runs towards an expected danger, and fake charges, where the rhino avoids a genuine assault, are normal protective ways of behaving.

   Understanding these ways of behaving is significant for carrying out compelling systems to moderate human-natural life struggle, guaranteeing the security of the two rhinos and nearby networks.

8. **Reactions to Dangers: Flight, Battle, or Freeze**

   Rhinoceroses display a scope of reactions when confronted with dangers, and these reactions are frequently connected to their developmental history as prey creatures. Flight is a typical reaction, where rhinos might take off from an apparent risk. Be that as it may, when departure is absurd, rhinos might fall back on battle or freeze ways of behaving.

   The battle reaction includes utilizing their strong bodies and impressive horns to shield themselves. The freeze reaction, where a rhino stops and evaluates what is happening, is a more careful methodology. Understanding these reactions is vital for the security of the two rhinos and those functioning in protection, as well with respect to creating compelling enemy of poaching measures.

9. **Preservation Difficulties: Human Effect and Conduct Changes**

The protection of rhinoceroses is unpredictably connected to understanding and addressing the provokes they face because of human exercises. Poaching for rhino horns, territory misfortune, and human-natural life struggle are huge dangers that can impact rhino conduct. Expanded pressure, adjusted development examples, and changes in friendly designs are seen in rhino populaces confronting such difficulties.

Preservation endeavors should consider the social transformations expected to adapt to these dangers and work towards establishing conditions where rhinos can show their regular ways of behaving without unjustifiable unsettling influences.

10. **Protection Methodologies: Coordinating Social Exploration**

Coordinating conduct investigation into preservation systems is fundamental for the outcome of rhino protection programs. Conduct studies give basic bits of knowledge into the requirements of rhinos, the effect of preservation intercessions, and the adequacy of defensive measures.

Utilizing telemetry, camera traps, and direct perception, analysts can screen rhino conduct, development examples, and reactions to protection intercessions. This data illuminates versatile administration techniques, guaranteeing that protection endeavors line up with the regular ways of behaving and prerequisites of rhino populaces.

11. **Eco-The travel industry: Adjusting Preservation and Guest Experience**

Eco-the travel industry has arisen as a possible device for rhino preservation, giving subsidizing to defensive measures while offering guests the valuable chance to observe these wonderful animals in their normal territories.

Notwithstanding, overseeing eco-the travel industry requires a sensitive equilibrium to forestall adverse consequences on rhino conduct, like adjustment to human presence or interruptions to social designs.

Dependable eco-the travel industry rehearses accentuate negligible interruption, moral survey distances, and instructive drives to bring issues to light about the significance of saving rhino natural surroundings and ways of behaving.

12. **Future Exploration and Preservation Difficulties: A Comprehensive Methodology**

As moderates endeavor to get the eventual fate of rhinoceroses, progressing research and an all encompassing methodology are fundamental. Future investigations might dig further into the conduct nature of various rhino species, the effects of environmental change on their way of behaving, and the exchange between social variations and hereditary variety.

Preservation challenges, including poaching, living space fracture, and human-untamed life struggle, require interdisciplinary arrangements that think about both the organic and conduct parts of rhinoceros populaces. By getting it and regarding the social complexities of rhinos, preservationists can foster viable techniques that guarantee the proceeded with endurance of these notable species.

6.2 Significance of body language in communication

Correspondence is a complex interaction that stretches out past verbal articulation, including a rich embroidery of non-verbal signs known as non-verbal communication. From the unobtrusive flash of an eyebrow to the certain step of a speaker, these non-verbal signs assume a urgent part in conveying feelings, expectations, and relational elements. This extensive investigation digs into the significant meaning of non-verbal communication in correspondence, unwinding its effect on connections, proficient associations, multifaceted comprehension, and the complexities of human articulation.

1. **The Quiet Orchestra of Non-Verbal Articulation**

   Non-verbal communication, frequently alluded to as the quiet orchestra of correspondence, includes the utilization of signals, looks, stances, and developments to pass on messages without words. This quiet language works on an inner mind level, impacting how people see and answer each other. The subtleties of non-verbal communication add profundity, setting, and close to home reverberation to verbal correspondence, making a more extravagant and more nuanced type of articulation.

2. **Comprehensiveness and Social Subtleties**

   While specific parts of non-verbal communication display all inclusiveness, social subtleties altogether shape its translation. Generally perceived looks, for example, a grin demonstrating joy or wrinkled temples flagging concern, rise above social limits. In any case, the significance appended to explicit signals or stances might shift across societies. Attention to social subtleties in non-verbal communication is fundamental for viable diverse correspondence, forestalling misconceptions and encouraging social ability.

3. **Looks: Windows to Feelings**

   Looks are maybe the most powerful and natural type of non-verbal correspondence. The human face can convey an immense scope of feelings — from satisfaction and shock to outrage and bitterness. Microexpressions, momentary facial developments enduring parts of a second, give looks into real feelings that people might endeavor to intentionally disguise. The capacity to translate looks upgrades the ability to appreciate anyone on a profound level, empowering people to explore social communications with more prominent responsiveness and understanding.

4. **Motions: Upgrading Verbal Correspondence**

   Motions are indispensable to human correspondence, filling in as strong enhancements to verbal articulation. A lifted hand to imply an inquiry, a gesture to convey understanding, or a wave to welcome somebody — these motions improve and explain verbal messages. While certain signals have widespread implications, others might be culture-explicit, stressing the requirement for mindfulness and versatility in assorted open settings.

5. **Stance and Body Developments: The Language structure of Presence**

   Stance and body developments add to the punctuation of non-verbal communication, forming the general message a singular passes on. A certain and open stance might flag confirmation, while slumping or shut non-verbal communication might propose frailty or inconvenience. Intentional developments, for example, inclining forward to communicate interest, make a powerful layer of correspondence that supplements and builds up verbal articulation.

6. **Eye to eye connection: Laying out Association and Trust**

   Eye to eye connection is a principal component of non-verbal correspondence that lays out association and encourages trust. Supported eye to eye connection during a discussion signals mindfulness, commitment, and truthfulness. On the other hand, staying away from eye to eye connection might convey distress, timidity, or an absence of certainty.

   In different societies, the assumptions about eye to eye connection contrast, highlighting the significance of understanding and regarding social standards in this part of non-verbal communication.

7. **Proxemics: Exploring Individual Space**

   Proxemics, the investigation of individual space, impacts how people explore their actual closeness to other people. Various societies have fluctuating standards and assumptions about private space, affecting the solace levels of people during associations. Understanding and regarding proxemics add to compelling correspondence, keeping distress or strain emerging from attack of individual space.

8. **Distinctions in sexual orientation in Non-verbal communication**

   Non-verbal communication is affected by cultural assumptions and standards, adding to unpretentious orientation explicit signals. From the manner in which people sit to the utilization of signals and articulations, there are frequently gendered designs implanted in non-verbal communication. Perceiving these subtleties is essential for destroying generalizations and advancing fair correspondence, permitting people to articulate their thoughts legitimately without adjusting to unbending cultural contents.

9. **Non-Verbal Correspondence in Proficient Settings**

   In proficient settings, non-verbal correspondence assumes a huge part in forming view of skill, authority, and dependability. Certain stance, confident handshakes, and kept in touch can add to positive impressions, while squirming or staying away from eye to eye connection might convey vulnerability or absence of certainty. Dominance of expert non-verbal communication improves one's viability in work environment correspondence and relational connections.

10. **Misleading Non-verbal communication: Figuring out a deeper, hidden meaning**

    While non-verbal communication frequently lines up with authentic contemplations and feelings, people may likewise utilize misleading non-verbal communication to cover their actual sentiments or aims. Conflicting motions, constrained grins, or staying away from eye to eye connection can be signs of double dealing. Perceiving these signs, frequently alluded to as "tells," is fundamental for knowing realness in relational collaborations, dealings, and compromise.

11. **Non-verbal communication in Connections: The Dance of Closeness**

    In personal connections, non-verbal communication turns into a nuanced dance that conveys love, fondness, and association. From the delicate hint of a hand to the unobtrusive slant of the head, couples foster their own quiet language that extends close to home bonds. On the other hand, negative non-verbal communication, like crossed arms or dismissed act, can flag pressure or separation. Supporting positive non-verbal communication is fundamental to building and supporting sound connections.

12. **The Effect of Innovation: Computerized Non-verbal communication**

    In the period of advanced correspondence, non-verbal communication reaches out into the virtual domain. Computerized non-verbal communication includes components like emoticons, accentuation, and the tone of composed messages. The shortfall of looks and actual signals presents difficulties, expecting people to be aware of their computerized non-verbal communication to convey feelings precisely and forestall false impressions in web-based associations.

13. **Upgrading Relational abilities: The Craft of Careful Articulation**

    Creating compelling relational abilities includes developing care in both verbal and non-verbal articulation. Focusing on one's own non-verbal communication, being receptive to the non-verbal signals of others, and rehearsing undivided attention add to upgraded relational correspondence. The craft of careful articulation includes adjusting verbal and non-verbal messages to make bona fide, conscious, and compassionate communications.

14. **Public Speaking: Bridling the Force of Presence**

    In broad daylight communicating in, dominating non-verbal communication is instrumental in drawing in, convincing, and spellbinding a group of people.

From certain steps in front of an audience to deliberate signals that accentuate central issues, compelling speakers saddle the force of non-verbal communication to convey authority and associate with their audience members. The organization of presence through non-verbal communication is an expertise that can be sharpened to leave an enduring effect on crowds.

15. **Social Capability and Inclusivity**

Social capability in deciphering and utilizing non-verbal communication is fundamental for cultivating comprehensive and successful correspondence. Consciousness of different social standards and assumptions forestalls misinterpretations and guarantees that non-verbal signs are grasped in setting.

In multicultural settings, people who exhibit social capability in their non-verbal communication add to a comprehensive climate that values variety.

16. **Non-verbal communication in Compromise**

Non-verbal communication assumes a urgent part in compromise, impacting the tone and result of talks. Open and harmless non-verbal communication can de-heighten strains, while cautious or forceful stances might intensify clashes. Talented mediators focus on both verbal and non-verbal prompts, utilizing non-verbal communication decisively to fabricate affinity, lay out trust, and work with valuable discourse.

17. **The Job of Mirror Neurons: Compassion and Association**

Reflect neurons, particular cells in the mind, assume a part in the reflecting of others' activities and feelings. This brain reflecting adds to compassion, permitting people to comprehend and interface with the encounters of others. With regards to non-verbal communication, reflect neurons work with a common close to home insight, encouraging a feeling of association and compatibility between communicators.

18. **Non-Verbal Correspondence in Training**

In instructive settings, non-verbal correspondence is a powerful part of the educating and growing experience. Instructors use signals, looks, and non-verbal communication to convey energy, explain ideas, and draw in understudies. Essentially, understudies express their grasping, interest, or distress through their own non-verbal communication. Instructors who are sensitive to non-verbal prompts make a more responsive and comprehensive learning climate.

19. **Non-Verbal Correspondence in Medical care**

In medical services, non-verbal correspondence is necessary to patient consideration and supplier patient connections. Medical care experts use non-verbal communication to convey compassion, console patients, and lay out trust. Patients, thusly, express agony, inconvenience, or appreciation through their own non-verbal prompts. Compelling non-verbal correspondence upgrades the nature of care, adds to patient fulfillment, and cultivates a positive medical services climate.

20. **Moral Contemplations: Regarding Limits and Assent**

    Moral correspondence includes regarding individual limits and acquiring assent, especially in the domain of non-verbal signs. Contact, closeness, and certain motions can have various implications for people in view of their social foundation, individual encounters, or solace levels. Moral communicators explore these subtleties with responsiveness, guaranteeing that their non-verbal communication is conscious and lines up with the inclinations and limits of others.

21. **Advanced Non-verbal communication in the Work environment**

    As the working environment develops with remote and half and half models, advanced non-verbal communication turns out to be progressively important. Virtual gatherings, messages, and coordinated effort stages request another arrangement of advanced relational abilities. Attention to advanced non-verbal communication remembers contemplations of tone for composed correspondence, camera presence in video gatherings, and the utilization of emoticons to precisely convey feelings. Creating capability in computerized non-verbal communication is fundamental for successful virtual coordinated effort and correspondence.

22. **Web-based Entertainment and Visual Correspondence**

    Virtual entertainment stages influence visual correspondence, depending on pictures, recordings, and viewable signs to pass on messages. People curate their computerized personas through profile pictures, emoticons, and the decision of visual substance. The effect of visual correspondence via online entertainment reaches out indeed, forming discernments and connections in the advanced scene.

23. **Non-verbal communication and Close to home Guideline**

    Non-verbal communication is firmly connected to profound guideline, affecting how people express and deal with their feelings. Cognizant control of non-verbal communication can add to close to home guideline by forestalling the accidental movement of feelings that may not line up with the planned message. The capacity to control non-verbal communication improves the ability to understand people on a deeper level, cultivating successful correspondence in different settings.

24. **Neurodiversity and Non-Verbal Correspondence**

    Perceiving and regarding neurodiversity includes understanding that people might have different non-verbal correspondence inclinations and styles. A few people on the mental imbalance range, for instance, may communicate their thoughts through special non-verbal communication or have aversions to specific non-verbal prompts. Establishing comprehensive conditions includes adjusting correspondence ways to deal with oblige neurodiverse points of view and inclinations.

25. **Non-Verbal Correspondence in Augmented Experience**

As innovation propels, augmented reality (VR) acquaints new aspects with non-verbal correspondence. Symbols in virtual spaces can convey signals, articulations, and non-verbal communication, recreating a more vivid and reasonable type of correspondence. Understanding the subtleties of non-verbal correspondence in computer generated experience becomes pivotal as these stages reshape the manner in which people interface and team up in advanced conditions.

26. **Moral Contemplations in Observation and Protection**

In a period of observation innovation, moral contemplations emerge concerning the utilization of non-verbal communication for checking and examination. Reconnaissance frameworks that track and dissect people's developments and articulations raise security concerns. Moral practices include straightforward correspondence, informed assent, and dependable utilization of observation advancements to defend people's freedoms and independence.

27. **Creating Non-verbal communication Mindfulness: Preparing and Training**

Upgrading non-verbal communication mindfulness includes schooling and preparing drives that outfit people with the abilities to really decipher and utilize non-verbal prompts. Correspondence courses, studios, and assets on non-verbal communication engage people to turn out to be more capable communicators, cultivating positive connections in private and expert settings.

28. **Challenges in Deciphering Non-verbal communication**

While non-verbal communication is an amazing asset for correspondence, difficulties might emerge in its understanding. Social contrasts, individual varieties, and setting explicit prompts can prompt misconceptions. Continuous exploration and training are fundamental for fostering a nuanced comprehension of non-verbal communication and refining understanding abilities to explore complex informative situations.

29. **Self-awareness and Self-Reflection**

A singular's non-verbal communication reflects their correspondence with others as well as their interior state and self-discernment. Taking part in self-reflection and developing mindfulness of one's own non-verbal communication add to self-awareness. Understanding how non-verbal communication lines up with feelings, expectations, and correspondence objectives engages people to convey genuineness and fabricate significant associations.

6.3 Interactions within rhinoceros social structures

Rhinoceroses, notorious monsters of the savannas and woods, show mind boggling social designs that assume an essential part in their endurance and prosperity. While social ways of behaving fluctuate among various rhinoceros species, these connections give a brief look into the helpful elements, specialized strategies, and progressive designs inside their networks. This investigation dives into the entrancing domain of rhinoceros social designs, revealing insight into the intricate trap of connections that characterize their lives.

1. White Rhinoceros Accidents: Agreeable Living

White rhinoceroses (Ceratotherium simum) are known for shaping bigger gatherings called crashes. An accident ordinarily comprises of a few people, frequently drove by a prevailing male known as a bull. Inside the accident, an organized order arises, with females and their calves framing the center gathering. Helpful residing is a sign of white rhinoceros social designs, where people team up to guarantee the security and prosperity of the gathering.

Inside a white rhinoceros crash, cooperations are set apart by correspondence through vocalizations, non-verbal communication, and common preparing. These ways of behaving fortify social securities, add to the foundation of a dominance hierarchy, and cultivate a feeling of local area among people. The helpful idea of white rhinoceros social designs improves their capacity to safeguard against hunters and explore the difficulties of their surroundings.

2. Dark Rhinoceros Isolation: The Puzzler of Lone Living

Rather than the gregarious idea of white rhinoceroses, dark rhinoceroses (Diceros bicornis) are for the most part more single in their social designs. While they might meet up for the purpose of mating, dark rhinos are known for their autonomous and regional ways of behaving. Cooperations inside dark rhinoceros networks are in many cases brief and spin around romance and mating.

Regional ways of behaving assume a huge part in the communications among dark rhinos. Male dark rhinos, specifically, mark their regions with excrement heaps and pee to convey proprietorship and limits. Brief experiences between people might happen, particularly during mating season, yet drawn out friendly connections are more uncommon. The baffling idea of dark rhinoceros isolation features the variety of social designs inside the rhinoceros family.

3. Correspondence Through Vocalizations: The Rhinoceros Language

Correspondence inside rhinoceros social designs includes a scope of vocalizations that pass on data about mind-set, expectations, and possible dangers. Rhinos produce snorts, grunts, and blares, which act as a type of the rhinoceros language. These vocalizations are especially significant during communications inside the gathering, assisting people with remaining associated and coordinate their developments.

Calves speak with their moms through unmistakable calls, making a bond that is significant for their endurance. Predominant bulls might utilize vocalizations to attest their strength or express their presence to different rhinos nearby. Understanding the rhinoceros language is fundamental for scientists and moderates trying to unravel the subtleties of rhino correspondence and conduct.

4. Regional Ways of behaving: Characterizing Limits and Assets

Regional ways of behaving are conspicuous in the cooperations inside rhinoceros social designs, particularly among dark rhinos. Laying out and guarding domains is pivotal for tying down admittance to fundamental assets like food, water, and reasonable rearing regions. Male rhinos, specifically, take part in regional ways of behaving, denoting their limits with compost and pee to convey possession.

Regional debates between rhinos, particularly guys, can prompt showdowns. These collaborations include presentations of predominance, vocalizations, and, now and again, actual conflicts. Understanding the elements of regional ways of behaving gives experiences into how rhinos explore and coincide inside their environments, guaranteeing the maintainability of their populaces.

5. Romance and Mating Customs: Personal Cooperations

Communications inside rhinoceros social designs become especially articulated during romance and mating customs. Mating ways of behaving include elaborate presentations, vocalizations, and actual collaborations among guys and females. Females might show open ways of behaving, demonstrating their status to mate, while guys take part in romance presentations to draw in expected mates.

Romance and mating customs are basic for the regenerative outcome of rhino populaces. These communications add to the hereditary variety of the species and guarantee the continuation of sound populaces. Noticing these personal collaborations gives specialists significant experiences into the conceptive ways of behaving of rhinoceroses.

6. Parental Consideration and Family Bonds: Supporting the Future

Inside rhinoceros social designs, parental consideration and family bonds are essential parts of their agreeable living. Female rhinos, particularly, are mindful moms, giving consideration and insurance to their calves. The solid connection among moms and calves adds to the endurance and prosperity of the more youthful individuals from the gathering.

Noticing parental consideration inside rhinoceros networks uncovers the supporting side of these strong creatures. Calves gain fundamental abilities from their moms, including scrounging methods, correspondence prompts, and techniques for exploring their surroundings. The family bonds produced inside rhinoceros social designs make a strong structure for the development and improvement of the future.

7. Pecking orders: Organizing Social Request

Pecking orders are obvious in associations inside rhinoceros social designs, especially in accidents of white rhinoceroses. Prevailing guys, or bulls, frequently lead the gathering, attesting their power through vocalizations, non-verbal communication, and actual showcases. Females inside the accident might lay out their own various leveled request in view old enough and strength.

Understanding pecking orders gives significant bits of knowledge into the social elements of rhinoceros networks. These designs assist with limiting struggles, lay out request inside the gathering, and add to the general union of the accident. Predominance isn't exclusively founded on actual strength; relational abilities and social knowledge additionally assume critical parts in forming progressive positions.

8. Social Learning and Transformation: Shared Information

Associations inside rhinoceros social designs work with social learning and transformation. More youthful individuals from the gathering, particularly calves, master fundamental abilities by noticing and copying the ways of behaving of more seasoned, more experienced people. From rummaging strategies to correspondence signs, social learning adds to the transmission of information inside the rhinoceros local area.

Transformation to ecological changes is additionally worked with through cooperations inside the gathering. Rhinos might share data about food sources, water areas, and expected dangers, adding to the aggregate strength of the local area. The capacity to adjust and gain from each other improves the endurance chances of rhinoceros populaces in unique environments.

9. Difficulties to Social Designs: Human Effect and Preservation Endeavors

Associations inside rhinoceros social designs face difficulties because of human effect, including natural surroundings misfortune, poaching, and human-untamed life struggle. These difficulties can disturb social elements, lead to pressure inside the gathering, and effect regenerative ways of behaving. Preservation endeavors are essential in relieving these difficulties and protecting the normal cooperations that characterize rhinoceros social designs.

Preservation drives center around making safeguarded territories, carrying out enemy of poaching measures, and limiting human-natural life struggle to shield rhinoceros populaces. By addressing the outer dangers to their social designs, moderates add to the support of sound and flourishing rhinoceros networks.

10. Protection Techniques: Figuring out Friendly Elements

Successful protection techniques require a profound comprehension of the social elements inside rhinoceros networks. Scientists utilize progressed methods, for example, telemetry, camera traps, and direct perception to screen social collaborations, development designs, and conduct transformations. This data illuminates preservation endeavors by adjusting intercessions to the regular ways of behaving and needs of rhinoceros populaces.

Coordinating conduct examination into protection procedures guarantees that endeavors are custom-made to the exceptional necessities of various rhinoceros species. By taking into account the complexities of their social designs, traditionalists can carry out measures that help the prosperity of rhinos and add to the manageability of their populaces.

11. Eco-The travel industry and Rhinoceros Social Designs

Eco-the travel industry has arisen as an expected device for rhino protection, offering valuable open doors for people to notice and value rhinoceros social designs in their normal environments. Mindful eco-the travel industry rehearses focus on negligible interruption, moral review distances, and instructive drives to bring issues to light about the significance of safeguarding rhino territories and ways of behaving.

While eco-the travel industry can offer monetary help for protection endeavors, cautious administration is fundamental to forestall adverse consequences on rhinoceros social designs. Progressives endeavor to find some kind of harmony that considers maintainable the travel industry while regarding the protection and regular ways of behaving of rhinos in nature.

12. Future Exploration: Disentangling More Secrets

As analysts keep on diving into the intricacies of rhinoceros social designs, future examinations might uncover extra secrets and subtleties. Examinations concerning the specialized techniques, social insight, and flexibility of rhinos can add to a more thorough comprehension of their way of behaving. Investigating the job of individual characters inside rhino networks and the effect of ecological changes on friendly designs are regions ready for additional investigation.

Chapter 7

Threats To Rhinoceros Anatomy

Rhinoceroses, with their famous horns and solid forms, face a huge number of dangers that risk their reality as well as the respectability of their life structures. These magnificent animals, containing different species, are standing up to an emergency driven by human exercises, natural changes, and a complicated trap of interconnected difficulties. This investigation digs into the dangers to rhinoceros life structures, inspecting the elements that jeopardize their actual prosperity and the protection endeavors pointed toward shielding these amazing species.

****1. Poaching and the Unlawful Untamed life Exchange: The Horn Issue**

Maybe the most quick and extreme danger to rhinoceros life structures is poaching, driven prevalently by the interest for rhino horns in unlawful natural life exchange markets. Rhino horns, made predominantly out of keratin — a similar substance tracked down in human hair and nails — hold social importance in some conventional medication rehearses and are erroneously accepted to have restorative properties.

Poachers savagely target rhinos for their horns, bringing about the grisly demonstration of dehorning, where the horn is effectively gotten rid of. This training, however pointed toward saving the rhinos' lives, presents dangers and difficulties to their life structures. The rhino's horn is in excess of a simple member; it serves different environmental capabilities, including protection, regional checking, and social collaborations. Dehorning can upset these normal ways of behaving, influencing the general life systems and conduct of the rhinoceros.

Preservation endeavors frequently include dehorning as a defensive measure, yet the moral and environmental ramifications of this training are subjects of continuous discussion. Finding some kind of harmony between safeguarding rhinos from poaching and protecting the uprightness of their life systems stays a perplexing test for protectionists.

2. Living space Misfortune and Discontinuity: Disturbances to Regular Life systems

Environment misfortune and discontinuity address inescapable dangers to rhinoceros life systems, influencing their normal ways of behaving, development examples, and by and large prosperity. As human populaces grow and scenes go through changes for horticulture, urbanization, and foundation advancement, rhino natural surroundings shrivel and become divided.

For rhinos, keeping up with tremendous and interconnected regions is critical for finding reasonable taking care of grounds, reproducing regions, and asylum from likely dangers. Discontinuity upsets these normal ways of behaving, prompting expanded human-untamed life struggle, limited development, and disconnection of populaces. Such interruptions can have flowing impacts on the life structures of rhinoceros species, affecting their actual wellbeing, conceptive examples, and long haul endurance.

Preservation techniques pointed toward moderating living space misfortune and discontinuity include laying out and keeping up with safeguarded regions, untamed life hallways, and supportable land-use rehearses. These actions look to shield the normal life systems of rhinoceros populaces by protecting the environments they rely upon.

3. Environmental Change: Moving Conditions and Transformation Difficulties

Environmental change represents an approaching danger to rhinoceros life systems by modifying the conditions they occupy. Changes in temperature, precipitation examples, and vegetation conveyance can affect the accessibility of food and water assets, influencing the general wellbeing and life structures of rhinoceros populaces.

Transformation challenges emerge as rhinos face shifts in their living spaces and the dispersion of plant species they depend on for sustenance. Drawn out dry spells, changed precipitation examples, and temperature limits can prompt food shortage and lack of hydration, affecting the physiological prosperity of rhinos. Also, environmental change might add to the spread of sicknesses that influence rhinoceros life systems and generally wellbeing.

Preservation drives tending to environmental change influences include checking natural changes, carrying out living space rebuilding undertakings, and creating techniques to help rhinos in adjusting to moving biological systems. By understanding the associations between environmental change and rhinoceros life structures, progressives can pursue guaranteeing the flexibility of these species even with ecological difficulties.

4. Illness Episodes: Subverting Wellbeing and Physiology

Illness episodes represent a huge danger to the life systems and in general strength of rhinoceros populaces. Irresistible illnesses, frequently exacerbated by factors like environmental change and natural surroundings debasement, can spread quickly among rhinos, prompting physiological pressure, debilitated safe frameworks, and, in extreme cases, mortality.

One model is the danger presented by ox-like tuberculosis, which can influence both hostage and wild rhinoceros populaces. The effect of sicknesses on rhinoceros life systems is complex, incorporating organ capability, regenerative wellbeing, and generally physiological versatility.

Protection endeavors center around sickness checking, preventive measures, and research to figure out the particular weaknesses of rhinos to different microbes.

5. Human-Untamed life Struggle: Physical and Mental Stressors

As human populaces infringe upon rhino territories, clashes among people and rhinos heighten, presenting dangers to the life structures and conduct of these brilliant animals. Human-untamed life struggle frequently brings about pressure for rhinos, appearing in modified physiological states, disturbed social designs, and possible wounds.

Rhinos might experience actual obstructions, for example, walls or streets, prompting wounds and stress as they explore modified scenes. The mental cost of consistent experiences with people, including the aggravation brought about by human exercises and the presence of settlements, can influence the normal way of behaving and life systems of rhinos.

Protection methodologies tending to human-untamed life struggle incorporate local area based drives, living space the board, and the improvement of reasonable practices that limit negative connections. By relieving clashes, traditionalists intend to protect the normal ways of behaving and physical prosperity of rhinoceros populaces.

6. Hereditary Variety: Suggestions for Life systems and Flexibility

Hereditary variety is a basic part of rhinoceros life systems, impacting the flexibility and versatility of populaces to ecological changes, infections, and different stressors. Diminished hereditary variety, frequently connected with little and segregated populaces, can prompt a higher gamble of hereditary issues, compromised safe frameworks, and diminished regenerative achievement.

The effect of hereditary variety on rhinoceros life structures stretches out past the singular level, influencing the general wellbeing and feasibility of populaces. Inbreeding sadness, coming about because of mating between firmly related people, can appear in different physical and physiological irregularities, undermining the drawn out endurance of rhino species.

Preservation endeavors to address hereditary variety incorporate procedures, for example, movements, which include moving people between populaces to present new hereditary material. These mediations plan to improve the versatile capability of rhinoceros populaces, guaranteeing the vigor of their life systems notwithstanding ecological difficulties.

7. Preservation and Hostile to Poaching Measures: Difficult exercise

While preservation and against poaching measures are fundamental for safeguarding rhinoceros life structures from the quick danger of unlawful untamed life exchange, they likewise present difficulties and moral contemplations.

Dehorning, a methodology utilized to hinder poachers, includes eliminating the rhino's horn to diminish its fairly estimated worth. While dehorning can save rhinos' lives, it raises worries about the effect on their life systems and normal ways of behaving.

The rhino's horn serves different biological capabilities, including guard, laying out predominance, and correspondence inside the gathering. Dehorning may disturb these ways of behaving, prompting changes in friendly designs and the rhinos' capacity to actually explore their surroundings. Finding some kind of harmony between shielding rhinos from poaching and saving the uprightness of their life structures stays a sensitive and continuous test for moderates.

8. Instructive Drives: Cultivating Concurrence and Understanding

Instructive drives assume a pivotal part in addressing dangers to rhinoceros life systems by cultivating concurrence among people and rhinos. By bringing issues to light about the significance of rhinos in biological systems, the dangers they face, and the job of life structures in their endurance, instructive projects engage networks to partake in preservation endeavors effectively.

Grasping the natural meaning of rhinoceros life systems, remembering their job for molding scenes and adding to biodiversity, urges networks to help protection measures. Taught people group are bound to participate in supportable practices, lessen human-untamed life struggle, and add to the drawn out safeguarding of rhinoceros populaces.

9. Innovation and Development: Instruments for Preservation

Headways in innovation and advancement offer important apparatuses for addressing dangers to rhinoceros life systems. From satellite following and telemetry to DNA examination, these apparatuses give progressives the resources to screen rhino populaces, grasp their developments, and carry out designated preservation procedures.

Robots and camera traps help in reconnaissance and observing endeavors, empowering progressives to follow rhino populaces, recognize criminal operations, and evaluate the effect of preservation mediations. Furthermore, hereditary advances take into consideration the evaluation of hereditary variety, illuminating movement endeavors to improve populace wellbeing.

10. Worldwide Joint effort: A Worldwide Way to deal with Preservation

The dangers to rhinoceros life systems rise above public lines, requiring global coordinated effort to actually address them. Worldwide drives, associations, and arrangements work with the sharing of information, assets, and ability among nations and associations committed to rhino preservation.

Worldwide cooperation upholds endeavors like enemy of poaching drives, territory insurance, and local area based preservation programs. By joining endeavors on a worldwide scale, progressives can use aggregate qualities to handle the multi-layered difficulties confronting rhinoceros life systems and guarantee the drawn out endurance of these notorious species.

11. Legitimate Structures and Strategy Support: Reinforcing Preservation

Viable preservation of rhinoceros life systems depends on powerful lawful structures and strategy promotion that address the main drivers of dangers. States, non-legislative associations (NGOs), and progressives cooperate to advocate for more grounded guidelines, punishments for poaching and unlawful untamed life exchange, and measures to safeguard rhino living spaces.

Strategy promotion likewise reaches out to resolving fundamental issues, for example, neediness, which can drive people to take part in criminal operations that hurt rhinos. By addressing the financial variables adding to dangers, moderates can establish a more reasonable and strong climate for rhinoceros populaces.

12. Economical Livelihoods and Local area Commitment: Engaging Nearby People group

Enabling nearby networks through reasonable occupations and local area commitment is an essential part of all encompassing rhino protection. By turning out elective revenue open doors, advancing supportable land-use rehearses, and including networks in preservation navigation, moderates encourage a feeling of responsibility and obligation to safeguarding rhinoceros life structures.

Feasible occupations lessen the dependence on exercises that hurt rhinos, like poaching or territory obliteration, while local area commitment constructs associations that benefit the two individuals and natural life. This approach perceives the interconnectedness of human prosperity and rhino protection, making a mutually beneficial situation for neighborhood networks and rhinoceros populaces the same.

7.1 Poaching and its impact on horn and hide preservation

The unlawful act of poaching, driven fundamentally by the interest for rhinoceros horns and stows away, represents an extreme and quick danger to the safeguarding of these famous animals and their complicated life structures. Rhinoceroses, with their particular horns and powerful stows away, face persevering double-dealing for their apparent restorative worth, decorative use, and social importance. This investigation digs into the complex effect of poaching on horn and conceal protection, looking at the environmental, monetary, and moral elements of this basic preservation challenge.

1. **The Horn Quandary: Abuse for Conventional Medication and Superficial points of interest**

   Rhinoceros horns, made essentially out of keratin, have for some time been desired in specific conventional medication rehearses, especially in pieces of Asia. In spite of lacking logical proof of any restorative properties, rhino horns are dishonestly accepted to fix different sicknesses, prompting their interest in unlawful business sectors. Also, the elaborate utilization of rhino horns as superficial points of interest further energizes the interest, fueling the danger to these grand creatures.

   The persevering quest for rhino horns for customary medication and superficial points of interest has desperate ramifications for horn conservation. Poachers frequently resort to fiercely dehorning live rhinos, a training pointed toward lessening the market worth of the horns and deflecting poaching. While dehorning may save the rhinos' lives, it raises moral worries and upsets the normal ways of behaving related with horn usefulness, like correspondence, regional stamping, and guard.

2. **Environmental Effect: Disturbance of Regular Ways of behaving and Biological system Elements**

Rhinoceros horns assume fundamental parts in the biological elements of their natural surroundings. The demonstration of poaching, whether through dehorning or killing rhinos for their horns, disturbs these normal ways of behaving and has flowing impacts on the more extensive biological system. The deficiency of rhinos, key herbivores in their environments, can prompt awkward nature in vegetation, influencing different species reliant upon these scenes.

Regional denoting, a fundamental way of behaving worked with by rhino horns, adds to social designs inside rhinoceros populaces. Poaching upsets these social elements, prompting likely contentions and changes in the various leveled request inside rhino networks. The deficiency of these regular ways of behaving influences the actual rhinos as well as resonates all through the multifaceted trap of connections inside their territories.

Moreover, the biological effect reaches out past rhinos to incorporate different species. Rhinos are known as cornerstone species, meaning they assume an excessively enormous part in molding and keeping up with the design of their environments. The downfall of rhino populaces because of poaching can meaningfully affect plant and creature species, disturbing the sensitive equilibrium that describes these regular habitats.

3. **Monetary Implications: The travel industry, Preservation, and Neighborhood People group**

The monetary repercussions of rhinoceros poaching resound across different areas, influencing the travel industry, preservation endeavors, and the vocations of nearby networks. Rhinos are appealling megafauna, drawing sightseers from around the world to observe these great animals in their normal living spaces. The deficiency of rhinos to poaching subverts the travel industry, which frequently fills in as an essential wellspring of income for nations with flourishing natural life populaces.

Protection endeavors, which require huge monetary assets, are stressed by the need to battle poaching and moderate its effects. Reserves that could be coordinated towards environment assurance, against poaching measures, and local area commitment are redirected to address the prompt emergency brought about by unlawful untamed life exchange. The monetary burden on protection drives hampers their capacity to carry out long haul procedures for the safeguarding of rhinoceros populaces.

Nearby people group that exist together with rhinoceros territories likewise bear the financial weight of poaching. Economical natural life the travel industry, when overseen dependably, can add to neighborhood economies through work creation and local area advancement. Notwithstanding, poaching risks these amazing open doors, prompting expanded human-natural life struggle as networks battle to track down elective types of revenue.

4. **Legitimate and Requirement Difficulties: A Worldwide Fight against Coordinated Wrongdoing**

The battle against rhinoceros poaching is compounded by lawful and requirement challenges, frequently described by transnational coordinated wrongdoing organizations. The unlawful exchange rhino horns is driven by refined criminal organizations that work across borders, taking advantage of shortcomings in legitimate structures and policing.

In certain areas, powerless lawful punishments for poaching and untamed life dealing add to the determination of these crimes. Poachers and dealers frequently work without risk of punishment, exploiting escape clauses in overall sets of laws and careless authorization. Reinforcing lawful structures, expanding punishments for untamed life violations, and upgrading worldwide collaboration are essential parts of the fight against rhino poaching.

Implementation endeavors, while essential, face critical difficulties in fighting very much subsidized and efficient crook organizations. The inclusion of defilement, pay off, and deficient assets further hampers the capacity of specialists to check poaching exercises really. The requirement for complete and composed worldwide endeavors to address these lawful and authorization challenges is central to the protection of rhino horns and stows away.

5. **Moral Contemplations: Dehorning and the Effect on Rhinoceros Life systems**

As a reaction to poaching, dehorning has arisen as a dubious protection system pointed toward shielding rhinoceroses from the prompt danger of unlawful natural life exchange. Dehorning includes the expulsion of the rhino's horn, diminishing its fairly estimated worth and making it less alluring to poachers. While dehorning can save rhinos' lives, it raises moral contemplations connected with the effect on rhinoceros life systems and conduct.

Rhinoceros horns serve different biological capabilities, including correspondence, regional stamping, and guard against hunters. Dehorning disturbs these regular ways of behaving, prompting changes in friendly designs inside rhino populaces. The evacuation of the horn might influence the rhinos' capacity to explore their surroundings, speak with each other, and attest predominance inside their gatherings.

Moreover, the demonstration of dehorning itself can be upsetting for rhinos.

The catch, sedation, and expulsion process present dangers to the prosperity of the creatures. The possible adverse consequences on rhinoceros life systems and conduct should be weighed against the prompt advantages of stopping poaching.

6. **Creative Preservation Systems: Innovation and Local area Inclusion**

   Despite the intricate test presented by rhinoceros poaching, imaginative preservation systems are fundamental. Innovation assumes a vital part in observing and safeguarding rhinos, with progressions like satellite following, robots, and camera traps giving significant devices to traditionalists.

   Satellite following empowers constant checking of rhino developments, permitting specialists to recognize uncommon ways of behaving that might show poaching dangers. Robots and camera traps give reconnaissance in far off regions, supporting the recognizable proof of poachers and the avoidance of criminal operations. These innovative headways upgrade the productivity and adequacy of against poaching endeavors, adding to the safeguarding of rhinoceros life systems.

   Local area inclusion is one more key component of imaginative protection methodologies. Drawing in nearby networks in rhino preservation endeavors cultivates a feeling of pride and obligation. By giving networks impetuses for safeguarding rhinos, like business potential open doors, training, and supportable livelihoods, protectionists make a cooperative methodology that benefits the two individuals and untamed life.

7. **Request Decrease Missions: Changing Discernments and Ways of behaving**

   Tending to the underlying driver of rhinoceros poaching requires handling the interest for rhino horns and stows away. Request decrease crusades center around changing discernments and ways of behaving connected with the utilization of rhino items, especially in conventional medication and fancy settings.

   Instruction and mindfulness drives advise shoppers about the need regarding logical proof supporting the restorative properties of rhino horns. These missions expect to disperse fantasies encompassing rhino items and energize the reception of elective materials in customary practices. By modifying customer conduct, request decrease endeavors add to the drawn out safeguarding of rhinoceros life structures.

   Worldwide joint efforts and associations with conventional medication professionals, local area pioneers, and compelling figures are critical in enhancing the effect of interest decrease crusades. These drives look to make a change in social perspectives towards rhino items, eventually diminishing the market request that drives poaching.

8. **Lawful and Strategy Promotion: Fortifying Insurances and Punishments**

   Backing for more grounded lawful insurances and punishments for poaching and untamed life dealing is a basic part of the more extensive preservation system. States, NGOs, and protection associations cooperate to campaign for administrative changes that improve the lawful system encompassing rhinoceros conservation.

Reinforcing lawful assurances incorporates shutting provisos that poachers exploit and guaranteeing that punishments for untamed life violations are comparable with the seriousness of the offenses. Promotion endeavors likewise reach out to global gatherings, asking nations to team up in the battle against transnational coordinated wrongdoing networks engaged with unlawful natural life exchange.

Strategy promotion envelops more extensive issues, for example, territory insurance, economical land-use practices, and local area based preservation drives. By impacting strategies at public and worldwide levels, advocates add to a thorough and incorporated way to deal with rhinoceros conservation.

9. **Preservation Financial matters: Esteeming Rhinos Alive**

Preservation financial matters centers around doling out monetary worth to living rhinos, underscoring the financial advantages got from their reality instead of their abuse. This approach perceives the environment administrations given by rhinos, including territory upkeep, biodiversity backing, and commitments to the travel industry income.

Esteeming rhinos alive makes financial motivators for networks to participate in preservation endeavors and safeguard these famous species. Income created from natural life the travel industry, directed safaris, and preservation arranged exercises adds to nearby economies, exhibiting the financial significance of saving rhinos as living elements.

Preservation financial matters additionally features the potential long haul monetary misfortunes related with the termination of rhinoceros populaces. The financial worth of rhinos stretches out past quick gains from poaching, underscoring the requirement for manageable and moral ways to deal with untamed life preservation.

10. **Worldwide Joint effort: Joined Against Poaching**

The battle against rhinoceros poaching requires a unified and worldwide exertion. Global cooperation is vital for address the transnational idea of unlawful natural life exchange and the complex organizations engaged with poaching exercises.

Worldwide coordinated efforts include sharing insight, assets, and mastery among nations, associations, and policing. Joint endeavors plan to reinforce hostile to poaching measures, work on lawful structures, and improve implementation capacities around the world. The sharing of best practices and examples learned adds to a more organized and viable reaction to the danger of rhinoceros poaching.

11. **Engaging Nearby People group: The Watchmen of Rhinos**

    Engaging nearby networks as stewards and watchmen of rhinos is essential in the preservation condition. At the point when networks are effectively engaged with rhino protection endeavors, they become accomplices in defending these species and their life systems.

    Local area strengthening drives remember giving schooling to natural life preservation, setting out work open doors in the eco-the travel industry area, and cultivating a feeling of satisfaction in safeguarding neighborhood biodiversity. By perceiving the job of neighborhood networks as vital to protection, these drives make a reasonable structure that benefits the two individuals and rhinos.

    Engaged people group act as an impediment to poaching exercises by going about as extra eyes and ears on the ground. Through joint effort with protection associations, legislatures, and NGOs, neighborhood networks become partners in the battle against rhinoceros poaching.

12. **Restoration and Renewed introduction: Modifying Rhino Populaces**

    Restoration and renewed introduction programs assume an essential part in re-making rhinoceros populaces that have been crushed by poaching. These drives include saving stranded rhino calves, restoring harmed people, and, now and again, once again introducing hostage reproduced rhinos into safeguarded environments.

    Recovery endeavors center around the physical and mental prosperity of protected rhinos, tending to wounds and injury brought about by poaching occurrences. Once restored, rhinos are painstakingly once again introduced into safeguarded regions, where they can add to the recuperation of wild populaces.

    Renewed introduction programs frequently include coordinated effort between preservation associations, natural life specialists, and nearby networks. Fruitful recovery and renewed introduction endeavors add to the revamping of rhino populaces and the protection of their life systems in regular habitats.

13. **Instructive Drives: Molding Future Stewards**

Instructive drives structure a foundation of preservation methodologies pointed toward tending to the main drivers of rhinoceros poaching. These projects target different crowds, including nearby networks, schools, and worldwide partners, fully intent on forming future stewards of untamed life and advancing a protection disapproved of ethos.

Schooling encourages a comprehension of the biological significance of rhinos, their job in biodiversity, and the dangers they face. By imparting a feeling of obligation and sympathy, instructive drives add to the drawn out conservation of rhinoceros life systems by making an age of people focused on safeguarding these superb animals.

Instructive effort stretches out past customary study hall settings to envelop computerized stages, narratives, and intuitive encounters. By utilizing different channels, instructive drives amplify their effect in bringing issues to light, evolving mentalities, and rousing aggregate activity for rhino preservation.

7.2 Habitat loss and its effects on rhinoceros populations

Natural surroundings misfortune, an outcome of human exercises like horticulture, urbanization, and foundation improvement, remains as one of the main dangers to rhinoceros populaces around the world. As these magnificent animals lose their normal natural surroundings, they face a bunch of difficulties that influence their endurance, conceptive examples, and generally prosperity. This investigation digs into the mind boggling issue of environment misfortune and its overwhelming consequences for rhinoceros populaces.

1. **Fracture and Segregation: Upsetting Regular Ways of behaving**

   One of the quick effects of environment misfortune is the fracture and detachment of rhinoceros populaces. As human exercises change scenes, rhino living spaces become progressively divided, prompting secluded pockets of populaces. This discontinuity upsets the regular development examples of rhinos, restricting their capacity to get to appropriate taking care of grounds, reproducing regions, and urgent assets.

   Disconnection can bring about hereditary bottlenecks, lessening the in general hereditary variety of rhinoceros populaces. With restricted open doors for quality stream between disengaged gatherings, inbreeding turns into a worry, possibly prompting hereditary irregularities, diminished conceptive achievement, and compromised resistant frameworks. The drawn out impacts of hereditary bottlenecks can present critical difficulties to the versatility and flexibility of rhinoceros populaces.

2. **Changed Taking care of and Searching Examples: Battle for Assets**

   Living space misfortune frequently means a decrease in accessible vegetation, influencing the taking care of and searching examples of rhinoceroses. As their regular territories recoil, rhinos might confront contest for restricted assets, including brushing regions and water sources. The battle for assets can prompt changes in the conveyance and conduct of rhinoceros populaces.

   For herbivorous rhinos, admittance to different plant species is fundamental for meeting their wholesome necessities. Living space misfortune might bring about the decay of favored plant species or the infringement of intrusive plants, influencing the quality and amount of accessible rummage. These progressions can have flowing consequences for the wellbeing, conceptive achievement, and by and large physiological prosperity of rhinoceroses.

3. **Expanded Human-Natural life Struggle: Dangers to Rhino Endurance**

   The infringement of human exercises into rhino environments frequently brings about expanded human-untamed life struggle. As rhinos lose their regular domains, they might wander into regions populated by people looking for food and water. This collaboration can prompt struggles that posture direct dangers to the endurance of rhinoceros populaces.

Human-untamed life struggle might include rhinos harming crops, causing property obliteration, or in any event, presenting dangers to human wellbeing. In counter, networks might fall back on destructive practices, for example, harming or shooting rhinos, fueling the dangers looked by these imperiled species. The heightening of human-untamed life struggle further imperils rhinoceros populaces previously wrestling with the difficulties of environment misfortune.

4. **Stress and Social Changes: Effect on Propagation**

The deficiency of their regular living spaces can expose rhinos to ongoing pressure, coming about because of expanded openness to human exercises, territory corruption, and the difficulties of adjusting to changed conditions. Stress can appear in conduct changes, influencing the conceptive examples of rhinoceros populaces.

In pressure prompting circumstances, rhinos might show modified conceptive ways of behaving, diminished fruitfulness, and disturbed mating customs. Female rhinos, specifically, may encounter postponed conceptive cycles or lower regenerative achievement, affecting the capacity of populaces to support themselves. The pressure related with natural surroundings misfortune adds an extra layer of intricacy to the preservation endeavors pointed toward saving rhinoceros populaces.

5. **Uprooting and Decline: Ramifications for Species Endurance**

As environment misfortune strengthens, rhinoceros populaces might confront dislodging from their conventional reaches. This relocation can bring about the development of little, secluded bunches with restricted admittance to reasonable natural surroundings. The outcomes of such fracture and decline are significant, with the gamble of nearby eliminations and a waning in general populace size.

Little and secluded populaces face increased weakness to outer dangers, including infection flare-ups, hereditary issues, and natural changes. The absence of hereditary variety in these populaces further lessens their versatile potential, making them vulnerable to the difficulties presented by a quickly impacting world. The decay of rhinoceros populaces because of environment misfortune raises worries about the drawn out endurance of these notable species.

6. **Protection Difficulties: Adjusting Human Necessities and Natural life Safeguarding**

Tending with the impacts of natural surroundings misfortune on rhinoceros populaces presents a considerable protection challenge that requires a fragile harmony between human necessities and untamed life conservation. Quick urbanization, horticultural extension, and framework advancement frequently drive environment misfortune, requiring cautious preparation and manageable land-use practices to moderate the effect on rhinos.

Protection drives should think about the concurrence of human networks and rhinoceros populaces. Executing measures like untamed life passages, safeguarded regions, and reasonable land the board practices can assist with mitigating the tensions of living space misfortune. Furthermore, people group commitment and training assume significant parts in encouraging comprehension and backing for protection endeavors, at last adding to the amicable conjunction of people and rhinos.

7. **Territory Reclamation: A Fundamental Protection Procedure**

Notwithstanding living space misfortune, natural surroundings rebuilding arises as a crucial protection procedure to relieve its consequences for rhinoceros populaces. Rebuilding endeavors include recovering debased environments, establishing local vegetation, and making hallways that interface divided scenes. These mediations expect to reestablish the normal equilibrium of biological systems and furnish rhinos with the assets they need for endurance.

Living space rebuilding benefits rhinoceros populaces as well as adds to the general strength of biological systems. By reproducing practical territories, progressives make spaces where rhinos can communicate their normal ways of behaving, keep up with solid conceptive examples, and add to the biodiversity of their surroundings.

8. **Worldwide Cooperation: A Bound together Exertion for Protection**

The conservation of rhinoceros populaces notwithstanding environment misfortune requires a bound together and worldwide exertion. Global joint effort among legislatures, protection associations, scientists, and neighborhood networks is fundamental for address the underlying drivers of territory misfortune and carry out maintainable arrangements.

Worldwide drives should focus on the security of basic rhino territories, advance dependable land-use rehearses, and participate in cooperative examination to more readily figure out the environmental requirements of rhinoceros populaces. By co-operating on a worldwide scale, partners can foster exhaustive procedures that defend the environments important for the endurance of rhinos.

7.3 Conservation efforts and initiatives

Notwithstanding raising dangers like poaching, natural surroundings misfortune, and human-untamed life struggle, deliberate protection endeavors and drives are urgent to guaranteeing the endurance of rhinoceros populaces. Preservationists, legislatures, neighborhood networks, and global associations have combined efforts to execute a scope of procedures pointed toward safeguarding these notable species. This investigation digs into the assorted and imaginative drives that structure the foundation of progressing preservation endeavors for rhinoceros populaces.

1. **Against Poaching Measures: Gatekeepers on the Cutting edges**

   Integral to rhinoceros protection is the execution of powerful enemy of poaching measures. Hostile to poaching endeavors include conveying gifted officers, utilizing innovation, for example, robots and camera traps, and utilizing knowledge organizations to screen and safeguard rhino populaces. Officers, frequently the overlooked yet truly great individuals of preservation, watch safeguarded regions, track rhinos, and block poachers before they can hurt these glorious animals.

   Notwithstanding boots on the ground, innovation assumes a significant part in enemy of poaching endeavors. Drones give airborne reconnaissance, covering tremendous scenes and recognizing dubious exercises. Camera traps catch pictures and information that guide in observing rhino developments and distinguishing expected dangers. These mechanical progressions upgrade the productivity and viability of hostile to poaching drives, going about as strategic advantages in the battle against unlawful untamed life exchange.

2. **Dehorning: A Moral Issue for Sure fire Assurance**

   To stop poaching and lessen the market worth of rhino horns, a few progressives resort to dehorning - the expulsion of rhino horns. While questionable because of its moral ramifications and possible effect on rhino conduct, dehorning has been utilized as a momentary methodology to safeguard rhinos from prompt dangers.

   Dehorning is performed via prepared veterinarians under controlled conditions to limit pressure and guarantee the prosperity of the rhinos. While it offers an impermanent respite from poaching, moral contemplations incorporate the possible interruption of regular ways of behaving related with horn usefulness, like correspondence and regional stamping. The discussion encompassing the ethicality and long haul adequacy of dehorning highlights the intricacy of protection navigation.

3. **Local area Based Protection: Encouraging Stewardship**

   Drawing in nearby networks as dynamic members in rhinoceros protection is fundamental to long haul achievement. Local area based preservation drives expect to encourage a feeling of stewardship by including nearby occupants in the security of rhino environments. This approach perceives the interconnectedness of human prosperity and natural life preservation, empowering networks to become partners in the battle against dangers to rhino populaces.

   Local area based preservation programs frequently incorporate instruction, work creation, and manageable occupation valuable open doors. By showing the unmistakable advantages of rhino preservation, for example, eco-the travel industry income and work valuable open doors, these drives fabricate a common obligation to defending these famous species. Furthermore, engaging neighborhood networks as overseers of rhino territories diminishes the probability of human-natural life struggle.

4. **Territory Reclamation: Recovering Fundamental Spaces**

As territory misfortune stays a huge danger to rhinoceros populaces, natural surroundings rebuilding drives assume a crucial part in preservation endeavors. These undertakings center around recovering corrupted living spaces, establishing local vegetation, and making natural life halls to reconnect divided scenes. By reestablishing practical environments, traditionalists give rhinos the assets they need to flourish, guaranteeing the protection of their normal ways of behaving and regenerative examples.

Environment rebuilding benefits rhinoceros populaces as well as adds to the general strength of biological systems. These drives make strong territories equipped for supporting a different exhibit of animal categories, building up the interconnected trap of life. Cooperative endeavors to reestablish and safeguard basic rhino territories are fundamental for the drawn out endurance of these radiant animals.

5. **Movement and Renewed introduction: Modifying Populaces**

In circumstances where rhino populaces face critical dangers or have declined, movement and renewed introduction programs become essential preservation apparatuses. These drives include moving rhinos from areas of high gamble to more secure natural surroundings, as well as once again introducing hostage reproduced rhinos into safeguarded scenes.

Movement endeavors require cautious preparation and coordination to limit weight on the rhinos and guarantee their fruitful variation to new conditions. Renewed introduction programs mean to reconstruct populaces in regions where rhinos have been extirpated, adding to the rebuilding of biological equilibrium. While these drives offer expect the recuperation of rhino populaces, they require continuous checking and versatile administration to address difficulties like poaching dangers and environment reasonableness.

6. **Exploration and Observing: Informed Preservation Techniques**

The outcome of preservation endeavors depends on a profound comprehension of rhinoceros science, conduct, and nature. Examination and checking drives give basic bits of knowledge that illuminate preservation methodologies and empower versatile administration. Researchers and scientists concentrate on rhino populaces, track developments, and survey the wellbeing and hereditary variety of people to successfully tailor protection mediations.

Innovative headways, like satellite following and hereditary investigation, improve the accuracy and extent of exploration endeavors. Observing the progress of preservation measures, figuring out populace elements, and distinguishing arising dangers add to prove based navigation. A very much educated approach guarantees that assets are dispensed in an intelligent way, boosting the effect of preservation drives.

7. **Worldwide Cooperation: A Worldwide Reaction to Worldwide Difficulties**
   Given the transnational idea of the dangers confronting rhinoceros populaces, global coordinated effort is central. Legislatures, non-administrative associations (NGOs), and preservation offices from around the world unite to share aptitude, assets, and best practices. Cooperative drives include facilitated enemy of poaching endeavors, research organizations, and the trading of information to address the complicated difficulties of rhino protection.
   Global cooperation stretches out to strategy support and conciliatory endeavors pointed toward reinforcing legitimate systems and improving requirement against unlawful natural life exchange. By cooperating, nations can enhance their effect, influence aggregate assets, and encourage a bound together reaction to the worldwide difficulties undermining rhinoceros populaces.

8. **Instruction and Mindfulness: Forming Protection Values**

Schooling and mindfulness drives structure a foundation of rhinoceros preservation by molding values, encouraging compassion, and imparting a feeling of obligation. Focusing on assorted crowds, from nearby networks to worldwide partners, these drives convey the natural significance of rhinos, the dangers they face, and the job people can play in their safeguarding.

Through instructive projects, narratives, and effort exercises, preservationists mean to make a groundswell of help for rhino security. Mindfulness crusades likewise assume an essential part in combatting interest for rhino items, dissipating legends encompassing their therapeutic properties, and advancing moral and supportable decisions.